INCLUSIVE POPULISM

CONTENDING MODERNITIES

Series editors: Ebrahim Moosa, Atalia Omer, and Scott Appleby

As a collaboration between the Contending Modernities initiative and the University of Notre Dame Press, the Contending Modernities series seeks, through publications engaging multiple disciplines, to generate new knowledge and greater understanding of the ways in which religious traditions and secular actors encounter and engage each other in the modern world. Books in this series may include monographs, co-authored volumes, and tightly themed edited collections.

The series will include works that frame such encounters through the lens of "modernity." The range of themes treated in the series might include war, peace, human rights, nationalism, refugees and migrants, development practice, pluralism, religious literacy, political theology, ethics, multi- and intercultural dynamics, sexual politics, gender justice, and postcolonial and decolonial studies.

INCLUSIVE
POPULISM

Creating Citizens
in the Global Age

ANGUS RITCHIE

University of Notre Dame Press
Notre Dame, Indiana

University of Notre Dame Press
Notre Dame, Indiana 46556
undpress.nd.edu

Published in the United States of America

Library of Congress Control Number: 2019021580

ISBN: 978-0-268-10577-8 (hardback)
ISBN: 978-0-268-10578-5 (paperback)
ISBN: 978-0-268-10580-8 (WebPDF)
ISBN: 978-0-268-10579-2 (Epub)

∞ This book is printed on acid-free paper

For Jennifer

CONTENTS

Preface   ix
Acknowledgments   xiii

ONE   A Populist Moment   1

TWO   Community Organizing as Inclusive Populism   27

THREE   Engaging the Theoretical Debate I:
           A Critique of Liberalism   59

FOUR   Community Organizing: Six Challenges   69

FIVE   Integration, Islam, and Immigration   105

SIX   Engaging the Theoretical Debate II:
           Traditions, Pluralism, and Populism   137

SEVEN   Inclusive Populism and the Renewal of Politics   147

           Notes   155
           Bibliography   171
           Index   175

PREFACE

Authors are usually delighted when the course of events makes their work more salient. But it is impossible to delight in the fact that, even as I have been writing this book, our democratic crisis has become more intense.

Inclusive Populism: Creating Citizens in the Global Age not only describes and diagnoses the current crisis; it charts a path to democratic renewal. The book offers an "up-close" account of how community organizing helps strangers to become fellow citizens, both through and for the tending of public life. This empirical study is interwoven with an engagement (particularly in chapters 3 and 6) with the relevant theoretical debates. By these means it argues that the rise of "fake populisms" on right and left alike is a symptom of more fundamental weaknesses in secularizing liberalism and that community organizing is a practical example of a constructive alternative that I have called "inclusive populism." A striking feature of this alternative is that it draws on the diverse religious and ethical traditions in Western democracies and the institutions that embody and promote them. Indeed, it understands these institutions to be vital to the formation of democratic citizens.

The work has its origins in the University of Notre Dame's multidisciplinary Contending Modernities initiative, which aims to increase understanding of the ways in which religious and secular forces interact in the contemporary postsecular world. By engaging political theorists, theologians, ethicists, and social scientists in sustained conversation and deliberation, Contending Modernities explores two distinct narratives of the postsecular. One narrative holds that a process of secularization has occurred but that religion in our admittedly secular age is proving more resilient than many theorists had expected and is becoming interwoven with the secular in sometimes hidden, always creative, ways. The alternative narrative challenges the very idea of a "process of secularization," in part by pointing to the enduring influence of organized religion but also by noting the persistent and near-comprehensive sacralization of so-called "ordinary" spheres of life, from the economy and the state to personal identity and its burgeoning accoutrements. Contending Modernities sets these sometimes competing, sometimes overlapping, narratives within the overarching discourse of modernity.

Narratives of both the secular and the religious inform the argument of this book, which addresses and attempts to interpret a context in which religion looms considerably larger in politics than secularists would have hoped or expected only a few decades ago.

While the *Inclusive Populism* project is rooted in these theoretical debates, it seeks to inform public discourse and action. It also seeks to engage with voices that are usually marginalized from such conversations. To that end, this book draws on three main sources of material about community organizing, alongside the extant scholarly literature.

First, David Barclay (at the time a colleague at the Centre for Theology and Community) conducted twenty semistructured interviews with individuals from a wide variety of religious, ethnic, and cultural backgrounds. All of the interviewees have been involved in grassroots engagement across different religions and beliefs, most of them through work with Citizens UK, the national community organizing movement (and a sister organization to the Industrial Areas Foundation in the United States). The interviews lasted, on average, 45 minutes and explored, among other topics, the reasons interviewees were involved in their projects, whether and how their work enabled them to build meaningful relationships, and the ways their projects handled faith and other fundamental motivations. A small number of additional interviews were also conducted with academics who specialize in the areas of multiculturalism and faith in public life.

Second, three of my colleagues conducted a further forty interviews that explored the experiences and motivations of those involved in Citizens UK in London's most deprived neighborhoods and communities. Ruhana Ali and Caitlin Burbridge conducted interviews as part of their day-to-day work as community organizers in, respectively, the London Borough of Tower Hamlets and among London's Congolese Diaspora. In addition, theologian Arabella Milbank interviewed Christians from a range of denominations involved in The East London Citizens Organisation (TELCO), the local chapter of Citizens UK.

Third, I drew on two accounts written by religious leaders and community organizers in the United Kingdom and the United States of their experiences of and motivations for engagement in the practice. These accounts are published in two collections, *Effective Organising for Congregational Renewal* and *A New Covenant of Virtue*.[1]

The purpose of the various first-person accounts collected through these interviews and written accounts is to enable those involved in the practice of community organizing to speak in their own words and on their own terms. Alongside this range of interviews and testimonies, I have added insights from my own experience of two decades of ministry in East London parishes involved in Citizens UK.

Inclusive Populism was written in and for the present moment, which is the product of a unique confluence of factors. Alongside the rise in the "fake populisms" of right and left and the increasing interest in the practice of community organizing as an authentic alternative, the year 2013 saw the election of a pope whose theology and practice are rooted in the experience of the poorest. One of the most admired public figures in the world, Pope Francis has spoken powerfully about the damage done to the common good when billions of people are systematically marginalized. The most authentic Christian theology, he insists, emerges from and informs the experience of struggle. Pope Francis's vision of a theology and politics rooted in the lives of the poorest citizens is an important inspiration for this book.

The present political and religious moment will eventually pass. The deep-seated flaws in our liberal political order, however, are structural, and we will be living with their debilitating effects for some time to come. It is my hope that the political and social vision embraced by *Inclusive Populism* will be of enduring relevance.

ACKNOWLEDGMENTS

I want to begin by thanking R. Scott Appleby and Vincent D. Rougeau for their oversight of the research project that generated this book. I am grateful to Scott for his combination of patience, wisdom, and encouragement and to Vincent for over a decade of friendship and collaboration as we have explored (in this and other projects) the ways community organizing helps diverse communities to build a common life.

The research project is described in more detail in the preface, and I want to thank Ruhana Ali, David Barclay, Caitlin Burbridge, and Arabella Milbank for carrying out and writing up their interviews and for the earlier papers and reports of our project on which this book draws.

I am grateful to colleagues and friends who have read part or all of the text, among them Matthew Bolton, Ernesto Cortés, Simon Cuff, Hugo Foxwood, Joshua Harris, Neil Jameson, Jonathan Lange, Simon Mason, Claire Moll, Dan Rhodes, Dunstan Rodrigues, Richard Springer, Selina Stone, Tim Thorlby, Ralph Walker, and Andy Walton. In particular, the advice of Philip Krinks has (on this, as on many other occasions) proved invaluable.

The book describes a particular, embodied practice of "inclusive populism"—and so I want to recognize and thank the people and institutions that are part of the community organizing movement. I am deeply grateful to the members of the congregations in which I have ministered in East London (the Parish of the Divine Compassion, Plaistow and North Canning Town in Newham, and St. Peter's Bethnal Green and St. George-in-the-East in Tower Hamlets); the trustees and staff of the Centre for Theology and Community (in particular our Chaplain Sister Josephine Canny); and the community organizers with whom I have worked in Citizens UK (in particular Neil Jameson as he retires from an extraordinarily fruitful thirty years as its founding director) and its sister alliances around the world.

I also want to offer heartfelt thanks to Stephen Little, Marilyn Martin, and all those at the University of Notre Dame Press who have contributed to the production of the book.

While the weaknesses in this work remain my own, I owe each of the people I have mentioned a debt of gratitude for making it possible.

This book is dedicated to my wife, Jennifer. The process of researching and writing *Inclusive Populism* began a month after our wedding and has included the first five years of our son Callum's life—and the first four months of Euan's. I am hugely grateful for all the love that is given and received in our life together and for the patience and support Jennifer has provided during the researching and writing of this book.

CHAPTER I

A Populist Moment

The first day of May 2017 was a poignant anniversary. Twenty years earlier, Tony Blair had swept to power as prime minister of Britain in a landslide victory, proclaiming a "new dawn" in UK politics. His sense of optimism reflected the wider temper of the times. Bill Clinton had just been inaugurated for a second term as US president, and Boris Yeltsin was serving as the first democratically elected leader of the Russian Federation.

These memories stood in painful contrast with the political scene two decades later. In Britain, Blair's vision of a "modern," multicultural nation anchored in the European Union buckled under the weight of wars in Afghanistan and Iraq and successive social and economic convulsions. It was finally put to rest on 23 June 2016, when a narrow majority of Britons voted to leave the European Union after a campaign dominated by the fear of immigration and the perceived need to "take back control" from foreigners.

Across the Atlantic, the change in political mood has been even starker. The angry nativism of Donald Trump's campaign for president represented a departure from the hopeful and inclusive optimism of Barack Obama's "Yes, We Can" campaign eight years earlier. On the day of his inauguration, the new president declared that his predecessors of both parties had presided over an "American carnage."[1] The divisive tone of Trump's rhetoric—and policies— has shaped his presidency thus far.

Perhaps the one thing that unifies an otherwise deeply fractured America is this mood of anger and anxiety. As the new president was delivering his inauguration address, a wave of "women's marches" two million strong protested his election. Marking the first anniversary of the inauguration and the protest, an equal or larger number of outraged citizens again took to the streets calling for resistance to the administration.[2]

While Trump proclaimed "America First," he understood that his rise was part of a new political reality sweeping across many nations. In his campaign he repeatedly invoked the Brexit vote in Britain and argued for a more positive relationship with Russian President Vladimir Putin. In the early days of his administration, he endorsed the far-right candidate Marine Le Pen in her contest with Emmanuel Macron for the French presidency. While the United States, the United Kingdom, France, and Russia are very different contexts, the rise of right-wing populism seemed an international phenomenon. Across a range of contexts, it manifested striking commonalities: a hostility to "liberal elites" and democratic norms, the proclamation of a "clash of civilizations" between Christianity and Islam, and a deep hostility to immigration, which is blamed for the dilution of each country's "Christian heritage." Increasingly, across these different contexts, fellow citizens are being turned into strangers.

Three factors help to explain this rise in far-right populism: the increasing flows of global migration, the resultant increase in religious diversity, and a period of intense economic upheaval whose cost has been distributed unevenly.

Across the world, twenty cities include among their residents more than one million migrants. Together, these cities, which are the epicenters of global wealth and power, contain one in five of the world's migrants, as well as standing at the heart of the flows of global migration.[3]

The majority of these cities lie in historically Christian countries. With the exception of Russia (where the Soviet regime sought for many decades to impose atheism on the populace), all of these countries are undergoing a decline in religious belief and practice. Now, however, global migration is bringing religiously committed new citizens into these nations—many of them adherents of Christianity and Islam. The reason is simple: While these two faiths make up around half of the world's total population, it is estimated that they account for three-quarters of the world's migrants.[4] Ironically, in 1966, just as Harvey Cox was writing *The Secular City*, which called attention to patterns of urbanization that seemed at the time postreligious, these flows of global migration began to increase dramatically. They have helped put religion back on the agenda of western political debate and rendered Cox's narrative of "secularization" problematic.[5]

As for pressures exerted by failing economies, Russia entered a period of economic crisis in the final years of the 20th century. The welfare and employment protections of the former Soviet Union were dismantled at a time when a new capitalist elite was engaged in conspicuous consumption. In the West, the financial crash of 2008 generated a similar dissonance, with the restaurants and boutiques of the wealthiest areas recovering quickly while the majority of citizens endured a sustained period of stagnant wages and reduced public services. Putin's rise to power, Britain's Brexit vote, and Trump's election came on the heels of their nations' respective economic upheavals.

SECULARIZING LIBERALISM AND INCLUSIVE POPULISM

The failure of political leaders across the spectrum to respond effectively to these demographic, religious, and economic shifts has exposed the underlying inadequacies of an approach to politics I term "secularizing liberalism." In this book I explore these inadequacies and explain why the current "populisms" of right and left are flawed responses. Notwithstanding their ideological differences, these two so-called populisms share a common weakness. Neither the liberal activism of the left nor the authoritarian nationalism of the right is rooted in the lives of the people it claims to represent. This book proposes a humane and effective alternative—a truly inclusive populism that unites diverse citizens in action for the common good.

It is important to begin by characterizing this diversity accurately. Following the Commission on Religion and Belief in British Public Life (CoRAB), I use the French term *convictions* for these citizens' different religions and beliefs. As the Commission explains:

> In international legal documentation the equivalent of the English phrase *religion and belief* is in French *la religion et les convictions*. The French word *convictions* has connotations of firmness, weight, intensity and commitment and refers to something which is fundamental

in someone's sense of values, self-worth and identity. To count as a belief so far as the law is concerned, a point of view or *une conviction* must "attain a certain level of cogency, seriousness, cohesion and importance, be worthy of respect in a democratic society and . . . not incompatible with human dignity."

Belief in the sense of *les convictions* has close similarities with religion. It . . . can be a way of feeling connected to others, can give a sense of meaning and significance, can be a source of narratives, stories, symbols and teachings which impart moral guidance and inspiration, can build courage and resilience in times of trouble, can be a place of ceremony at times of celebration or grief, and can motivate acts of kindness, compassion and generosity.[6]

As an empirical observation, citizens' diverse *convictions* evidently influence the political choices many of them make—thus shaping the laws and the behavior of governments. What I am calling a "pluralist" vision of politics is comfortable with these *convictions* being articulated in political debate. In one sense, a pluralist polity may or may not be "secular" (for it may or may not identify the state with any particular set of religious symbols), but it will not be "secularizing" (for it *will* allow citizens to bring their substantive convictions—including their diverse conceptions of the good life for individuals and communities—into the public square).

I use the term "secularizing liberalism" in contrast with such a pluralism. Whenever the text of the book refers to "liberalism" it means a vision of political discourse in which arguments must be made, and policies justified, in language that does not appeal to any specific *convictions* of this kind.

In place of secularizing liberalism, this book makes the case for an *inclusive populism*. This is an approach to politics rooted in the agency and the diverse *convictions* of citizens experiencing social injustice, from recent migrants to people in long-established working-class communities. I will argue that such a populist vision is embodied in the practice of broad-based community organizing.

As Pope Francis has observed, "populism" has very different meanings in different contexts: "In Latin America, it means that the people—for instance, people's movements—are the protagonists. They are self-organized. When I started to hear about populism in Europe I didn't know what to make of it, until I realized that it had different meanings." In Francis's words, 1930s Germany represented a disordered form of populism in which people did not "talk among themselves" but rather sought refuge from their fears in a "charismatic leader."[7] This dynamic is replicated in what might with justice be called the "fake populism" of our own times. It is fake because (unlike the people's movements praised by Pope Francis) it does not grow out of the experience or agency of ordinary citizens.

The contrast between the fake populism that is focused on a charismatic leader and the populism of self-organized citizens has some parallels with a distinction made by Luke Bretherton. In *Resurrecting Democracy* he distinguishes "anti-political populism," in which citizens "withdraw from public life to pursue private interests," from "political populism," which "embodies a conception of politics that works to reinstate plurality and inhibit totalizing monopolies (whether of the state or market) through common action and deliberation, premised on personal participation in and responsibility for tending public life."[8]

This book does not just argue for inclusive populism as an idea but claims that it is exemplified by the practice of community organizing.[9] It traces its development from the work of its founder, Saul Alinsky, in the slums of 1930s Chicago to the present-day work of the Industrial Areas Foundation (which Alinsky founded to spread the work across the United States) and its British sister organization, Citizens UK.

Drawing on the existing literature on community organizing and presenting new research on its impact in the deprived and diverse communities of inner-city London, I will show how the practice is an expression of inclusive populism and, in particular, how it helps the diverse communities brought together by global migration to build solidarity and trust, through and for the tending of public life.[10]

Global Migration and Religious Diversity

At this juncture it is important to set forth some empirical evidence about the relationship between global migration and the religious composition of many democratic nations.

The twenty-first century's patterns of migration differ in two vital respects from the previous waves of global migration, which occurred at the turn of the nineteenth and twentieth centuries. First, they occur in a context of proliferating legal obstacles to immigration. Before World War I, most mass migrations took place without visas, quotas, asylum status, smuggled illegals, or security barriers. After World War II, such requirements and restrictions on the flows of migrants began to appear; today, they are institutionalized and codified to an unprecedented degree.[11] Second, today's immigrants experience a greater level of ongoing systemic poverty and disadvantage than did those who migrated earlier. An International Monetary Fund briefing published at the turn of the twenty-first century reported, for example, that US immigrant males earned 4.1 percent more than native-born males in 1960 but 16.3 percent less in 1990. Immigrants always suffer an earnings disadvantage before they assimilate, but their initial wage (relative to that of the native-born) deteriorated by 24 percentage points between 1960 and 1990. Although the average educational attainment of immigrants improved, it did not increase as rapidly as that of the native-born.[12]

Recent global migration has four striking qualities. First, the cities and nations in which economic, political, and cultural power is concentrated have experienced massive flows of immigration. Second, the proportion of Christians and Muslims migrating is higher than the proportion of Christians and Muslims in the wider population. Moreover, those migrating often have a vibrant and passionate religious faith. Christianity and Islam are missionary religions, and the dominant traditions in both understand their doctrines to have implications for public life, as well as the "private morality" and "personal spirituality" of the believer. Third, the mass migration of religious believers to these previously secularizing urban areas is slowing down or perhaps even reversing the secular trend. Finally, this late twentieth-/early twenty-first-century wave of global migration is being discouraged by the policies of receiving nations, leading to a deepening of economic and educational disadvantage among migrants.

Any discussion of faith in public life in today's democracies needs to engage with the reality of sizeable migrant communities in these powerful cities, which are both religiously diverse and religiously committed, about immigration policy. The reality of existing migration cannot be wished away. Whatever the future shape of immigration policy, these democracies will have to learn to live well with the migration that has already occurred. In the unlikely event that all such countries decided to cap immigration at zero, and the even less likely event that such a cap would be enforceable, an urgent public challenge would remain: How to build a vibrant and peaceable common life in the midst of the deep religious and cultural differences that already exist.

Engaging constructively with Islam presents a particular challenge to these democracies. In most cases, prior to fairly recent flows of migration, the religious context has been largely one of a declining Christian population and a growing number of people who practice no religion. In such contexts, many have found it plausible to confine religion to a private "devotional" sphere and to suggest that the formulation of public policy be done on the basis of arguments that make no reference to such convictions.[13]

Many Christians have been party to the relegation of religion to the private sphere. As I argue in chapter 3, this is indefensible, regardless of the proportion of the population that is religious. Indeed, many Christian migrants come from cultures less influenced by the Western tendency to relegate religion in this way.[14] The forms of Islam dominant in migrant communities are particularly incompatible with the relegation of religion to a purely private realm. This fact raises urgent questions about how the convictions of the growing number of Muslim citizens are to be engaged with by the wider polity.

IMMIGRATION, RELIGION, AND THE NARRATIVE OF THE RIGHT

The evidence presented above is at odds with the narrative of right-wing populism. On both sides of the Atlantic, its politicians and commentators frequently deploy the language of their nation's being "a Christian country." This is frequently combined with hostility to immigration, often with the explicit implication that global migration is diluting the country's Christian character.[15]

Such claims, which appear regularly in the British media, are demonstrably false. Whatever the merits or demerits of Labour's relatively relaxed immigration policy between 1997 and 2010, it clearly had a positive impact on the number of practicing Christians. The striking decline in Christian practice and identification has little or nothing to do with immigration. Rather, the primary cause of decline is changing patterns of belief and identity in the indigenous population.[16]

The gap between the rates of Christian practice and identification among those over 60 and among those under 30 means that (even on the most optimistic assumptions about evangelism and church-planting initiatives) the reduction in numbers is unlikely to reverse in the near future.

The religious landscape in the United States is broadly similar. Again, the fundamental threat to the resilience of Christian practice of the country comes from the secularization of white citizens—who are more likely to be religiously unaffiliated than African Americans or Hispanics. Across the generations, the rise in affiliation to other faiths (which has risen from 4 percent to 8 percent of the population across half a century) is dwarfed by the rise in those who are unaffiliated (from 11 percent to 36 percent in the same period).[17]

The populist right on both sides of the Atlantic is therefore mistaken in its diagnosis. Immigration, far from eroding each country's Christian heritage, is often slowing—and in some neighborhoods reversing—the erosion. Underneath this surface anxiety, which is empirically mistaken, there are two deeper concerns about immigration. First, as in the case of most major flows of migration throughout history, members of host communities have anxieties about their economic security, specifically their job prospects and access to affordable housing. They also fear cultural change. Migrants may be more likely to be Christian than the host community, but the way in which that faith is understood and expressed may be very different. Second, there is a particular anxiety around Muslim immigrants, one that recalls nativist reactions in past centuries to Irish Catholic immigrants. In both cases, there has been a concern that migrants have a loyalty to a religious body beyond the nation-state. In Britain, prejudice against Irish immigrants was also intensified by the terrorism of the Republican movement. Today, across the West, prejudice against Muslims rose dramatically after the terrorist attacks of Al-Qaeda and Da'esh.

As I will argue in chapter 5, talk of a "clash of civilizations" between Christianity and Islam is both misleading and counterproductive. The purpose of the random and brutal attacks by those who talk this way is to goad the majority of Westerners into precisely the reactions being advocated by right-wing populists, namely, the scapegoating of moderate Islam for these crimes, and the growth in the belief that Islam *in general* is incompatible with democracy.

It is not surprising that right-wing populism has been associated with a "post-truth" politics. Its analysis of events is undermined by the empirical realities, hence its distrust of "experts." Its analysis is inaccurate on almost every level: mistaken in its claim that migration is a threat to Christian culture, mistaken in the assertion that migration is an economic drain on the host countries, and mistaken in its desire to portray a clash of civilizations between Christianity and Islam. These mistakes are not simply intellectual errors. They are, all too often, a consequence of a deliberate and cynical manipulation of the facts. The aim is to generate a narrative that chimes with popular anger and anxiety without addressing the underlying issues. The policies of the Trump administration, and those advocated by the more right-wing advocates of Brexit in the United Kingdom, will not materially improve the condition of the angriest and most alienated citizens. Moreover, the language of a clash of civilizations never extends to any serious critique of Saudi Arabia's Wahabi regime, to which the Trump administration is seeking to sell arms in greater numbers than ever.

This so-called populism is now led by members of the very elites it claims to despise. Donald Trump was a property magnate, Nigel Farage a City trader, and Vladimir Putin a leading figure in the Soviet security services. Marine Le Pen is the daughter of a politician.

LIBERALISM AND THE RISE OF RIGHT-WING POPULISM

Recent political campaigns (most notably Trump's for the 2016 US presidential election) have been bewildering for liberals. No amount of argument, pointing out the evident contradictions in far-right populism, seems to have had any impact on his supporters. Despite this, some liberals still believe all that is needed is a more robust reassertion of their position—a "liberal fight-back" against the delusions and hypocrisies of the populists. In a range of interviews in the spring of 2017, Tony Blair vented his frustration at the inept way liberalism was being defended in the United Kingdom. He lamented a "frightening authoritarian populism" and claimed that it was encouraging a growing number of voters to "identify an enemy as the answer to what are essentially the problems of accelerated change." Blair argued for the need for a renewed "center-ground," restating the case for a globalist, free-market liberalism against both the populism of the right and the populism of the left (which, to his dismay, has at this point taken control of his Labour Party).[18]

This book offers a very different analysis. In it I argue that the triple pressures of global migration, terrorism, and the financial crisis have exposed rather than created the flaws of liberalism. Over a number of decades, the central debate in British and American politics has been between a redistributive liberalism (with intellectual roots in John Rawls) and the "small-state" liberalism of Robert Nozick.[19]

On the surface, the liberalisms of Rawls and Nozick are very different. But they share one crucial assumption. Both seek to exclude from public policy-making any substantive debate about what constitutes a good life. On both Rawls's and Nozick's conceptions of politics, the nation-state cannot be bound together by any substantive ethical vision. By promoting individual autonomy and agency to the exclusion of all other values, their liberalisms forbid citizens to use elective politics to discern and pursue a common good.[20] As Chantal Mouffe has argued, liberal political theory assigns a purely functional role to politics, whereas "agonistic" confrontation on substantive issues is in fact vital to a healthy democratic culture. It is by embracing such tension and plurality, rather than seeking to eliminate it, that "antagonisms can be 'tamed,' thanks to the establishment of institutions and practices through which the potential antagonism can be played out in an agonistic way."[21]

The dominance of liberalism has led to a curious incoherence in political language. Over the past few decades, political rhetoric on both sides of the Atlantic has combined strong appeals to patriotism with a striking reluctance to articulate any genuinely substantive common values. Alasdair MacIntyre captures this odd and unstable combination: "The modern nation-state, in whatever guise, is a dangerous and unmanageable institution, presenting itself on the one hand as a bureaucratic supplier of goods and services, which is always about to, but never actually does, give its clients value for money, and on the other as a repository of sacred values, which from time to time invites one to lay down one's life on its behalf. As I have remarked elsewhere, it is like being asked to die for the telephone company."[22]

While my argument draws on Mouffe's critique of liberalism, it rejects her negative view of the role of religion in political debate. For, as I will argue, religious institutions and convictions have an important role to play in moving us beyond liberalism's narrow, technocratic conception of politics. It is in no small part the secularizing aspect of liberalism that has created fertile soil for the growth of right-wing populism. I discuss the theoretical weaknesses of secularizing liberalism in more detail in chapter 3. These theoretical flaws have practical consequences—causing liberalism to exacerbate the very tensions and anxieties it is designed to resolve.

First, secularizing liberalism ignores the crucial mediating institutions—churches and mosques, synagogues, unions, and schools—that foster the vital habits of democratic culture. Civil society needs to play an active, mediating role between the individual and the state. The bonds of mutual concern that are needed to sustain a common life themselves require nurture. They cannot simply be taken for granted. For the outcomes of elections and referenda to have legitimacy among all citizens, they need to be understood as the product of a shared process of discernment, not the brute assertion of the interests of the majority over the rest. This requires not only a free and fair process of voting but the sustaining of a democratic culture between elections. Citizens need to be in relationships of solidarity and trust across societal differences and to have experience of negotiating these differences to discern and promote a common good.

Second, liberalism inevitably encourages different ethnoreligious groups to understand each other as competitors. The founding myth of secularizing liberalism is that the moral and spiritual sources of these groups need to be kept out of the public square because their admission into that square can lead only to irresolvable conflict. This encourages different ethnoreligious groups to understand one another as rivals—and to seek recognition within the language and concepts of liberalism.[23]

For those who hold them, religious beliefs are not simply a personal (or communal) possession that need to be defended against incursions from rival groups. Rather, they are insights into the nature of reality, and thus into the sources of individual and communal flourishing. This is true not only of religious beliefs but, more widely, of the *convictions* (whether religious or secular) that we all hold. Liberalism can understand these diverse worldviews only as rivalrous, as sources of discord that need to be prevented from entering into the public square for fear of one group's values being "imposed" on another.

Contrary to the assumptions of secularizing liberalism, these *convictions* can play a constructive role in politics. This is evident from the experience of diverse communities that organize together for justice. In this process, the moral sources of different faiths and cultures can become shared resources for the building of a common life. To assert this is not to claim that people of different religions and beliefs "all believe the same thing." There are substantive and irresolvable differences between these religions and beliefs. No amount of argument looks likely to lead to the mass of citizens agreeing to any one such worldview. But this does not condemn citizens to a destructive stand-off between these *convictions*. The practice of community organizing shows that these different worldviews can engage much more constructively. They can both be the source of ongoing debate and disagreement and provide the moral and spiritual resources for the discernment of a truly common good.

This observation leads us to the third unintended consequence of liberalism. The effect of excluding these moral sources is to disempower the poorest communities. For it is most of all in these (often least secularized) communities that religion provides a crucial resource in the fight for social justice. The experience of community organizing alliances in the United Kingdom and the United States suggests that the poorest citizens have not found their religions and beliefs to be mere competitors. Their moral and spiritual sources have in fact resourced a shared struggle against the overweening power of state and market.

The key economic campaigns of community organizing alliances such as London Citizens—for a living wage and affordable housing and against exploitative lending—can all be understood as forms of resistance to the power of state and market. Catholic and Protestant Christians, Jews, Muslims, and Secular Humanists have managed to unite, drawing on diverse and substantive conceptions of the good.[24] Far from being a fair way of mediating between their conceptions of the good, liberalism prevents them from harnessing the most powerful resource they have in resisting an overweening market and an all-too-compliant state. In so doing, liberalism has disadvantaged our poorest communities in their struggle against *both* the untrammelled market *and* the centralizing and technocratic power of the modern state.

These three failings of liberalism are intertwined, and they reinforce one another. It is no coincidence that the Living Wage campaign in East London grew out of the effects of low wages on family and community life. Churches, mosques, and trade unions initiated the campaign after a community listening exercise revealed the impact of parents having to hold down several part-time, insecure jobs. This placed pressure on family life, as parents had to choose between having enough time to spend with their children and earning enough money to provide for them. It also made it impossible for these parents to play a full part in their wider community. There was simply no time left in their week for volunteering and civic engagement.

Secularizing liberalism has thus created a vicious cycle of disempowerment. The mediating institutions that foster a democratic culture are overlooked in liberal political theory, and the moral and spiritual sources they draw on are ruled inadmissible in public discourse. The result is to weaken these institutions, institutions that are central to the ability of the poorest communities to secure decent wages and affordable homes and to resist predatory lenders. These economic pressures make it even harder for citizens to engage in any activity beyond work and childcare, further weakening the democratic culture. Such a cycle of political disempowerment and economic impoverishment has created the perfect conditions for far-right populism: an angry and resentful population whose members have fewer and fewer opportunities to engage in the mediating institutions that give them a positive experience of power.

ANOTHER LIBERALISM: THE FALSE POPULISM OF THE LEFT

The weakness of liberalism and the dishonesty of the populist right have created space for a new populism of the left. Many commentators have argued that the Occupy movement represented the first stirrings of a genuinely popular revolt against social injustice. At the time of this writing, politicians in sympathy with this movement have achieved a new prominence on both sides of the Atlantic. The surprising success of Jeremy Corbyn in the United Kingdom led many writers to hail a popular revolt against economic liberalism. The result has reinforced the suggestion that Bernie Sanders might have had more success against Donald Trump than Hillary Clinton, with her "establishment" liberalism.

However, this movement on the left shares many of the weaknesses of the false populism of the right. Despite its rhetoric, the resurgence of the left lacks roots in the communities most alienated and angered by decades of liberalism. As Laura Grattan observes, the demography of the Occupy movement is rooted in the middle class.[25] This is also true of electoral support for both Sanders and Corbyn: The voting patterns in the 2016 US presidential election and the 2017 UK general election both demonstrate that the left is becoming less effective at engaging working-class voters (both white and of color) than it used to be.[26]

This failure of the left flows from its acceptance of a liberal political framework (which is often obscured by its angry denunciation of liberal economics). Far from being a genuinely populist movement, the tendency represented by Occupy is a form of activism largely exercised *on behalf of* the poorest communities. By failing to engage with their values and convictions, it perpetuates their political disempowerment.

Why has the supposedly populist left failed to engage the poorest citizens? As our team was beginning its research in East London, the Occupy LSX camp pitched its tents outside St. Paul's Cathedral. Just a mile from London's poorest neighborhoods, the camp sought to hold the capital's financiers to account for the financial crisis that had impoverished so many citizens. With banners proclaiming "We are the 99%," the Occupiers tapped into a widespread feeling of injustice driven in part by the awareness that, while the living standards of the vast majority of citizens had been eroded by the financial crash of 2008, the financiers of the City of London (like those of Wall Street) had received huge bailouts from the state and appeared to be as wealthy as ever. For a brief period, the Occupy camp seemed to capture the attention, and focus the concerns, of a wide swath of British society. However, the camp was unable to turn that sense of grievance into positive political change. There were three reasons for that failure, weaknesses that are also present in the Occupy movement in the United States.

First, the Occupiers failed to value the mediating institutions that are vital to a vibrant democratic culture. Institutions (in particular, religious institutions) were deemed forces of conservatism and oppression. Outside St. Paul's Cathedral, the Occupiers made a big deal of their intention to conduct business very differently: through general assemblies that proceeded only by unanimous agreement and through a wider form of governance that rejected all hierarchies.

What this approach failed to recognize was the inescapability of institutions in human life. For an institution is *precisely* the set of structured relationships that emerge when human beings agree to be faithful to one another across time. That is what a Scout group, trade union, marriage, and mosque have in common. It is one of the characteristic myths of our liberal culture that such commitments restrict human freedom. In fact, they are what enable humans to realize some crucial goods. The abandonment of these institutions does not liberate citizens. Rather, it causes their lives and communities to be dominated even more by the institutions of the market. In rejecting these structures as oppressive, the Occupiers found themselves unable to engage with their poorer neighbors in East London (who, as we shall see, were already organizing for social justice through their churches, mosques, and schools). For the same reason, they could not organize their own activities in a sustainable way.

This blindness to the power of social and institutional commitments exemplifies a wider failing of the newly resurgent left. Its suspicion of institutions per se leads to the failure either to build anything sustainable across time or to build a movement unhealthily focused (as in the case of the populist right) on particular individuals.

The second weakness of the Occupiers was a flawed understanding of inclusion. As David Barclay observes, many left-wing activists will engage only with people who pass a set of "progressive tests"—agreeing with a predetermined list of "acceptable" views on issues such as gender and sexuality.[27] He writes: "There is a deep irony at the heart of the 'progressive' political movement that whilst outwardly championing tolerance and diversity, many of its adherents are, in fact, deeply judgmental and restrictive in who they will engage in public action with. . . . If taken to its logical conclusion it would rule out the possibility of being friends with anyone who disagrees on anything of fundamental importance (i.e. ultimately we should only be friends not only with people who like us but with people who are like us)."

"Inclusion," in the world of such activists, extends only to those with progressive views on a wide range of social issues. Those with "reactionary" views were not welcome in the Occupy movement—a key reason that the Occupiers were deeply ambivalent about engagement with organized religion. While the Occupiers claimed "We are the 99%," it was very clear that a large subset of that 99 percent were insufficiently progressive to be admitted to the movement in any practical way.

Barclay's argument is directed against misguided right-wing attempts to tackle Islamic extremism, as well as against left-wing activists. For both groups, the problem is the same: "By precluding any possibility of building political friendships with those considered 'beyond engagement,' large sections of society (and in particular religious groups) are condemned to a position of isolation. Compounding this issue is the lack of evidence that 'progressive tests' are in any way effective in transforming the undesirable behaviors or beliefs of those classed as unsuitable for partnership."[28]

As we saw above, recent migrants are disproportionately likely to be religious. The "large sections of society" that are excluded by the progressive tests of the left are, ironically, the very groups the left likes to lionize: ethnic minorities, recent migrants, and (more generally) "the poor." The progressive tests of America's Democrats and their hostility to religious concerns were large factors in Trump's victory in key states such as

Florida (where, despite his hostile rhetoric, he garnered a crucial number of Latino voters).

While the white working class may be more secularized, the greater prevalence among white working-class voters of socially conservative attitudes, along with a concomitant suspicion of left-wing cosmopolitanism, means that they fall foul of the same processes of exclusion. This has fueled working-class support for right-wing populists on both sides of the Atlantic. Because the new left lacks deep roots in these communities, it has been unable to address the legitimate concerns many working-class voters have about the impact of immigration. This relates not only to the effect of immigration on their access to housing and to jobs. It also relates to the impact a high rate of churn in population in a neighborhood can have on relationships of solidarity and trust. From their more privileged social position, left-wing activists have often (like so many mainstream liberals) dismissed such concerns as "bigotry." Such a response is deeply counterproductive. By failing to attend to the genuine concerns such citizens have about the impact of immigration, liberals and left-wing populists have created a situation in which only the populist right seems attentive to these citizens' understandable and deeply felt concerns.

As Larry Elliott has observed, the rhetoric of many on the British left is deeply conflicted—on the one hand lionizing the poor and on the other betraying a patronizing contempt for them when they do not express the appropriate "progressive" sentiments. He cites their attitude to the European Union referendum as an example—but what he says would apply equally to wider concerns among working-class voters about recent flows of immigration: "The liberal left's . . . demand that poor people have a voice . . . sits oddly, to say the least, with the idea that the result of the [Britain's] EU referendum should be overturned because the poor people who voted for Brexit didn't know what they were doing. Giving people a voice means giving people a voice. It doesn't mean giving people a voice only when they agree with you."[29] At the time of my writing, Jeremy Corbyn (unlike many of his left-liberal supporters) has been keen to honor the result of the EU referendum. However, his more general political stance has not been one that has connected with the concerns of a significant group of working-class voters—hence the combination in the 2017 general election of a substantial increase in the overall Labour vote and a swing away from the party among poorer, less educated voters and in constituencies that voted "Leave" in the 2016 referendum.[30]

The final failing of the populist left is an unwillingness to negotiate and compromise. One of the catchphrases of Occupy LSX was "We're Occupy: We don't negotiate." While this may have sounded admirably principled, an unwillingness to negotiate is all too often an unwillingness to relate in a way that will yield practical change.

As one East London priest observed: "My congregation aren't interested in the Occupy camp, because they don't believe it will make any difference to their lives." That priest had had more than a decade's engagement in community organizing—developing the poorest members of his congregation, from a wide range of ethnic backgrounds, to act with their Muslim and secular neighbors for affordable housing and a living wage. Precisely because his inner-city congregation was directly affected by low pay and substandard, overpriced housing, they *were* willing to negotiate and compromise in order to achieve material improvements in their conditions. By contrast, many of the Occupiers (for whom the struggle for social justice was understood as a struggle on behalf of others who were poor) did not directly suffer when their intransigent stance led to the failure of the campaign.

These three weaknesses—in Occupy and the wider left—are interrelated. The unwillingness of many on the secular left to work with existing mediating institutions (and, in particular, the churches and mosques that engage many of the poorest citizens in inner-city neighborhoods) flows from their adherence to progressive tests and to a conception of "inclusion" that is disproportionately *exclusive* of both migrants and the white working class. Precisely because many left-wing activists are wary of institutions, they exhibit an arrogance and political immaturity that subverts their professed goals. For it is in institutions that we learn to negotiate deep difference—to live together with those whose views annoy and offend us—and it is in institutions that we learn to negotiate and compromise in order to ensure that our values can be translated into practical action. The imperfection of our institutions is not something that can be avoided by the pursuit of greater ideological purity. It is a direct consequence of the imperfection of the human heart.

To eschew institutional life in the name of "progressive principles" is to value your own righteousness over the possibility of improving the lives of your neighbors. This goes some way toward explaining an otherwise puzzling political phenomenon that we see on both sides of the Atlantic: that those who claim to fight for the interests of the poor find it hard to gain their support at elections.

The populism of the left may offer a departure from the economic liberalism of recent decades. But (as I argue in more detail in chapter 6) it shares the assumptions of political liberalism: a resistance to the language of faith and the illusion of an inclusive politics that can somehow be neutral with respect to the religions and beliefs of its citizens. In consequence, it has thus far been unable to address the discontents powering the surge in right-wing populism.

COMMUNITY ORGANIZING

In this book I make the case for a different kind of populism, not only as a theoretical possibility but as an empirical reality. In chapter 2 I will describe the practice of community organizing in some of Britain's and America's most deprived and diverse neighborhoods and will contend that it exemplifies the inclusive populism we so urgently need.

While community organizing has its origins in 1930s Chicago, its contemporary incarnation has striking resonances with the vision of politics being articulated by Pope Francis. He has been critical both of free-market, secular liberalism and of the nativist populism of the right. The populism that he has praised is one rooted in the experience of the poorest and committed to engaging across difference. Crucially, it begins with realities, not simply ideas. As Francis argues in *Evangelii Gaudium*, "Realities simply are, whereas ideas are worked out. There has to be continuous dialogue between the two, lest ideas become detached from realities. It is dangerous to dwell in the realm of words alone, of images and rhetoric. So [an important] principle comes into play: realities are greater than ideas."[31]

As we have seen, the populism of the left often remains in the realm of words and ideals. The Occupy LSX camp took refuge in the symbolic reenactment of *ideals* without being willing to undertake the hard labor of engagement and compromise across difference that would have enabled those ideals to transform reality. What Pope Francis has both embodied and invited others to embody is a willingness to engage in face-to-face dialogue across deep differences—not simply to lionize the poor as a category of person deserving of a better life but to engage in a daily practice of organizing with them for social justice.

Francis has understood the poorest as the central *agents* in the struggle for a better society. In that sense, his vision is more deserving of

the term "populism" than the alternatives we considered above. Addressing a worldwide gathering of social movements in Bolivia, the pope said:

> What can I do as a craftsman, a street vendor, a trucker, a downtrod-
> den worker, if I don't even enjoy workers' rights? What can I do, a
> farmwife, a native woman, a fisher who can hardly fight the domina-
> tion of the big corporations? . . . A lot! . . . You, the lowly, the exploited,
> the poor and underprivileged, can do, and are doing, a lot. I would even
> say that the future of humanity is in great measure in your own hands,
> through your ability to organize and carry out creative alternatives,
> through your daily efforts to ensure the three "L's" (labor, lodging, land)
> and through your proactive participation in the great processes of
> change on the national, regional and global levels. Don't lose heart![32]

Community organizing, as it has evolved in the decades since Alinsky's death, has three key features that enable it to avoid the pitfalls of the
false populisms discussed above and to develop a form of politics in which
the poorest citizens have agency. First, it is *institution-based*. Community
organizing builds on the mediating institutions that already exist in civil
society. These institutions are an essential element of a democratic culture.
It is in voluntary associations such as churches, synagogues, and mosques
that citizens commit to regular, faithful engagement with people who are
different from them—engagement around a set of common goods or values. It is there that they learn the democratic habits of listening and negotiating and build relationships of solidarity and trust. Across almost a
century of community organizing, religious and secular organizers have
found them to be the most resilient and powerful institutions on which
to build what Ernesto Cortés calls "a graduate school to teach people
how to participate in politics and shape their communities' futures." As
he explains: "Citizens are formed through the process of organizing. It
requires institutions which can incubate this process by passing on the
habits, practices, and norms necessary for humans with different opinions
and temperaments to flourish together: to compromise, to talk to and not
just about one another, to act in the light of one another's views and needs
and not just unilaterally or selfishly."[33]

The idea that religious congregations help to form democratic citizens—ones who are capable of building solidarity and trust across difference—may seem counterintuitive. As we have seen, secularizing liberalism

regards religion as a source of social *division*. In recent years, especially in the narrative of the populist right, mosques have been depicted as breeding grounds for isolationist and extremist attitudes. However, two independent studies undertaken in the last decade suggest that religious congregations can play a crucial role in the development of healthy relationships across differences of ethnicity, age, and social class. In 2014, Britain's Social Integration Commission found that churches and other places of worship number among the most socially integrated institutions in the country.[34] Its report stated:

> Across all ethnicities, ages and income backgrounds and in both social and work contexts, our experiences of interacting with those who are different from us are likely to be positive. . . . When integration of diverse groups happens, it is associated with higher levels of trust. . . . Negative interactions with those who are different from us are associated with lower levels of trust. However, the effects of these negative interactions are greatly reduced if we also have more positive experiences. Positive interactions between Britons who are different make British people more positive and trusting of people who are also different in other ways.[35]

Research from International Centre for the Study of Radicalisation and Political Violence has shown that the process of Islamic radicalization largely consists of *detaching* people from their relationships in local mosques.[36] This suggests that, instead of problematizing mosques, an effective strategy for tackling extremism would actually be to help mosques to become better organized—and, in particular, to develop stronger relationships between the older, more conservative generation (whose members usually dominate mosque governance) and the younger generation (whose members have to negotiate a range of different cultures in daily life).

That religious congregations are a source of "social capital"—an important place for recruiting volunteers for social action and for encouraging civic engagement—has long been understood by governments. However, all too often, governmental "faith-based" or "civil society" initiatives have wanted to instrumentalize these institutions, harnessing their capacity for bringing people together while asking them to leave their distinctive beliefs and values "at the door" (a request inspired by the liberal suspicion of those beliefs as inherently problematic).

Harry Boyte critiques what he calls a "flawed civil society" approach—which sees its institutions as sources of volunteers rather than as repositories of traditions and values that should inform political debate and are crucial to the formation of active citizens. This approach, which I have argued is encouraged by secularizing liberalism, "assigns politics to the arena of government, consultants, lobbyists and experts, leaving ordinary citizens as helpers on the side. It also separates production, which it locates in the economic sector, from public life. As a result, citizenship is purified, stripped of power, interests and the institutions necessary for serious civic work."[37]

Community organizing is unusual in the way it invites institutions (including religious congregations) to become *more* articulate about their distinctive convictions and motivations. Organizing also has a focus on the development of its member institutions. Rather than simply drawing on the social capital congregations already have, the mission of community organizing alliances is to strengthen those institutions—developing their grassroots leadership *through* as well as *for* action.

Second, community organizing is *inclusive*. It eschews progressive tests and applies only a "relational test." Institutions in community organizing alliances must be willing to work with those who are different—churches with mosques and synagogues, religious congregations with community groups, trade unions, and schools. This inclusive approach explains its ability to engage at depth with diverse communities in the poorest areas. It also provides the best hope of tackling extremism.

The desire to impose progressive tests usually comes from an anxiety that "unacceptable" views will be contagious if others engage with them. This explains the popularity among left-wing activists of "no-platforming" and the creation of "safe spaces" in which citizens are not exposed to views they find upsetting. While such strategies may be needed in a limited number of cases, their increasing popularity, in fact, reduces the exposure of those with "unacceptable" views to other perspectives, reinforcing the very attitudes they are designed to combat. The experience of community organizing is that solidarity rather than prejudice is contagious when people engage in one-to-one relationship building and common action. Extreme attitudes are more likely to spread when those relationships are absent. This is why right-wing populism has tended to spread through the media rather than through face-to-face encounters and has been most virulent in areas where people do not know anyone from other faiths and cultures. By contrast, as our study of community organizing in East London shows, when people get to know one another across these boundaries, mutual respect and solidarity are fostered.

Third, community organizing is *interest-based*. Community organizers teach people to identify, discuss, and act on their shared "self-interest."[38] Paradoxically, it is precisely its focus on interests that enables community organizing to hold together a genuine diversity of viewpoints and to organize *with* and not just *for* the poorest citizens. Organizing around citizens' self-interest is not the same as organizing around their selfishness.

What organizers mean by "self-interest" is simply "the interests of the selves in question." Participants in community organizing are taught to identify their own and others' self-interest by asking the following questions:

- What relationships are central to this person's life?
- How do they spend their time and money, and why?
- What were the motivations for key decisions they have made?
- What institutions are they involved in, and why?

By asking these questions, organizers focus on the practical choices people have made and the reasons for them rather than encouraging conversations about abstract ideals that may or may not affect their daily lives.

FROM SECULARIZING LIBERALISM
TO NEGOTIATED PLURALISM

Liberalism and the so-called populisms of right and left are primarily expressed through political parties. The role of most citizens in this process is simply to endorse such parties on election day. By contrast, community organizing sees the primary focus of democratic politics as the day-to-day institutional life of civil society. The role of the state, in this conception of politics, is both to create the environment in which such civil society can flourish and to provide (or enable the provision of) those goods that voluntary associations cannot.

What implications does this, very different, conception of politics have for political parties and policy-makers? First, they need to be willing to let civil society take more initiative in public life. That is to say, they need to accord voluntary associations the same respect and access to decision-making that is already given to businesses. When business leaders seek to engage with government on an issue of concern, they are usually referred to politicians and civil servants with the power to make decisions on that issue. By contrast, engagement with civil society is usually left to "community engagement" officers, who have little access to power and little influence on policy-making.

In addition, as I shall argue in more detail in chapter 5, politicians should stop problematizing supposedly "hard-to-engage" communities— most notably made up of recent immigrants, Muslims, and the white working class. The tone of political discourse with respect to these communities is all too often hectoring: demanding from a position of distance and privilege that these communities change their behavior. Immigrants are told to integrate more fully; Muslims are both told to integrate and to be less tolerant of extremists in their midst; members of the white working class are told to be more welcoming of diversity. Precisely because policy-makers are distant from these communities, such prescriptions lack understanding of their distinctive experience and interests. As we shall see, a deeper understanding of those interests would suggest a very different set of policy prescriptions.

Rather than lecturing these communities from afar, there are practical steps that government could take to help diaspora communities engage with the wider society, to support mosques in developing better intergenerational internal relationships and deeper relationships with other local institutions, and to address the legitimate concerns of established working-class communities about the impact of more recent immigration on their neighborhoods.

Finally, and most fundamentally, the experience of community organizing suggests the possibility of a genuinely pluralist politics. Secularizing liberalism can conceive of only two alternatives: *either* the privileging of one particular worldview (be it that of Christianity, Islam, or Secular Humanism) in public life *or* the exclusion of all such worldviews (in the name of a false "neutrality"). Community organizing embodies a third alternative, which I am calling *negotiated pluralism*. In the practice of organizing, citizens are encouraged to bring the whole of their moral and spiritual worldview into public discourse and then to identify the areas in which these divergent worldviews can offer a basis for common action. The ability of community organizing to generate a substantive agenda of policies—policies that command support from a surprising range of religions and beliefs—shows the potential of this pluralist approach.

If we are to build a peaceable and constructive common life in the midst of deep difference, people with different worldviews must sustain a number of different conversations at the same time. There needs to be space for *debates* between people of different religions and beliefs, conversations in which each party seeks to persuade the others of the rational superiority of their own position. There is no reason that an embrace of pluralism should involve minimizing what is at stake in those disagreements. Equally, however, there are few grounds for hope that the continuation of these debates will lead to convergence on a single agreed worldview.

Alongside such debates, two other kinds of conversation will be necessary. The first we might call *witnessing*—that is, the sharing (in a less adversarial and polemical context than intellectual debates) of the ethical and spiritual resources different religions and beliefs bring to a particular issue. Such acts of witness are central to community organizing. Trust and understanding are built between often radically divergent religions and beliefs as participants explain why their own worldview motivates them to oppose low pay and exploitative lending, to work for affordable housing, or to be hospitable to refugees.

The process of such mutual witnessing leads to greater understanding and trust, but it can also change beliefs. In East London, for example, the witness of Muslims explaining how Qu'ranic texts inspire their opposition to exploitative lending helped to draw Christians involved in community organizing back to reflect on the Biblical prohibitions of usury and to reflect on what it might mean to contextualize and act on those texts today. Because the Bible has a different place in Christian theology than that of the Qu'ran in Islam, the process of reflection was rather different for Christians than for Muslims. But the fundamental point remains: A conversation that was about mutual witness rather than apologetics changed the way in which Christian participants thought and acted—in a way that made them more, and not less, faithful to their own Scriptures.

It would be hopelessly optimistic to imagine that conversations concerned with *mutual witness* could secure all the agreement needed to build a common life—just as it is all too evident that conversations that take the form of *debates* will not lead all reasonable people to agree on any one religion or belief. There is a third register in which people of different worldviews need to converse, that of *negotiation*. Like the other two, this conversation does not require agreed metaphysical foundations. Quite the opposite: It is the conversation that people with ongoing disagreements about those issues need to have to negotiate a peaceable common life. Precisely because it is a conversation across deep disagreement, its course cannot be charted in advance, and it is not guaranteed to succeed. This is why, in Mouffe's terminology, it is inevitably "agonistic," for it involves rejecting "the rationalist belief in the availability of a universal consensus based on reason."[39] Such negotiation is not a purely cerebral engagement; if agonism is not to collapse into antagonism, a stock of goodwill and trust is required, and these need to be constantly nurtured. Negotiated pluralism depends, therefore, on relationships as well as ideas.

The practice of community organizing focuses on two of these three registers of conversation, the kinds I have termed "mutual witnessing" and (to a lesser extent) "negotiation." The evidence of this book is that a surprising amount can be accomplished when a diverse group of citizens engage in these kinds of conversation and take action on issues of common concern.

The solidarity and trust that are built by action on common concerns create an environment in which the more difficult conversations are much more likely to have fruitful outcomes.

CONCLUSION

The crisis of our times is above all a crisis of relationship. The rise of right-wing populism is an assault on the qualities of solidarity and trust, which are essential for a healthy society. Its language—of angry nativism, exclusion and scapegoating—is turning fellow citizens into strangers.

A crisis of relationships requires a solution that is focused on the re-weaving of solidarity and trust. In this chapter I have argued that liberalism is incapable of this task. Indeed, the failings of liberalism have generated a climate of anger and intolerance on both sides of the Atlantic.

In the chapters that follow I will describe and evaluate community organizing as an embodiment of an alternative vision of politics (chapters 2 and 4) and also seek to offer a theoretical critique of liberalism (chapter 3).

Inclusive Populism does not argue for a neat system to replace the tidy (but flawed) certainties of secularizing liberalism. Rather, it argues that untidiness is essential in democratic politics, that the best we can do is maintain a conversation across deep difference and engage in practices that build mutual understanding and concern.

What should give us hope is not just a new *theory* of pluralism. Rather, as I argue in this book, we should be encouraged by the *practice* of so many citizens in our most deprived and diverse neighborhoods. Their actions show that strangers can indeed become fellow citizens, learning to trust and care for one another, and so to build a more just and peaceful common life.

CHAPTER 2

Community Organizing as Inclusive Populism

The more the security staff learned about the event, the more anxious they became. In the United Kingdom, few political gatherings had taken place on the scale of the six thousand–person London Citizens' Assembly of 2016. What really worried security staff was the revelation that most participants would be arriving in delegations from inner-city churches, mosques, and synagogues.

The combination of religion and politics is often seen as problematic. Moreover, the 2016 London Citizens' Assembly was being held in the midst of an unusually acrimonious election campaign, one in which religion was turning into a major issue. The campaign of Conservative candidate Zac Goldsmith sought to portray Sadiq Khan (his Labour opponent) as an Islamic extremist. This line of attack drew outrage not only from Khan's allies but from many leading Conservatives.[1] As the Conservative campaign faced allegations of Islamophobia, Labour's former mayor Ken Livingstone was accused of antisemitism after making remarks about Adolf Hitler and Zionism that eventually led to his suspension from the party.[2]

At the 2016 event, the fears of the security staff were not realized. The assembly demonstrated that, for thousands of ordinary worshipers, faith was in fact a wellspring of solidarity and common action. Roman Catholics processed to the event from a special Mass with the Bishop of

Brentwood; other Christians had held an ecumenical prayer vigil. As soon as the assembly ended, the auditorium was turned into the venue for both Mahgrib (Muslim evening prayers) and their Jewish counterpart, Marriv. In between these liturgies, people of faith were joined by a smaller number from secular institutions to hold the two main candidates for mayor to account. The unity of purpose displayed by the churches, synagogues, and mosques involved in the assembly contrasted sharply with the divisive rhetoric of Goldsmith and Livingstone.

In this chapter of the book, I will explain how community organizing develops this unity of purpose across deep differences of religion and belief. Chapter 1 offered a brief outline of community organizing, explaining that it seeks to build an inclusive alliance around the institutions and interests of local people. In this chapter I will paint a more detailed picture of the practice, explaining the distinctive features that enable it to build a genuinely populist movement. The analysis draws on the work of Saul Alinsky in 1930s Chicago, the development of the Industrial Areas Foundation under his successor Ed Chambers, and research on contemporary organizing on both sides of the Atlantic. It does not simply suggest that a more authentic and inclusive populism would be a good *idea*.[3] Rather, it demonstrates that community organizing *embodies* such a populism. In so doing it is therefore a practice from which our wider polity has something to learn.

THE REDISTRIBUTION OF POWER

At the heart of Alinsky's approach were two key convictions. He believed that the redistribution of power to the poorest citizens was a precondition of any serious relief of the injustice they experienced. And he was convinced that this power would not be redistributed without a struggle. These convictions led him to build a movement that was genuinely owned and controlled by some of America's poorest citizens. As Jay MacLeod observes: "Alinsky's breakthrough was to reverse the logic of paternalistic reform by wresting control away from the professional do-gooders and handing it over to the people they were supposed to help. Alinsky transformed community activism from the liberal, elite-led endeavour it had become around 1900 into something he hoped would be more hardheaded and democratic."[4]

This focus on "people power" was on display at the London Citizens' Assembly. Its power comes from its ability to unite citizens from a wide range of backgrounds in long-term public relationships. The six thousand citizens at the mayoral assembly were not isolated individuals. All were members of one or another of the 210 institutions that make up the alliance. Most had been involved in the extensive process of listening and negotiating that shaped London Citizens' specific proposals—in this case on affordable housing, the living wage, and safe passage for refugees.

It was only the power of the alliance that made the mayoral candidates endure the public scrutiny of a London Citizens' assembly. Community organizing involves a level of robust and systematic accountability that politicians rarely face from anyone other than their electoral opponents and journalists. Rather than countenance the extended speeches typically endured at a hustings event, London Citizens gave the candidates relatively short amounts of time in which to indicate whether or not they supported the alliance's key proposals. These responses were then further scrutinized by grassroots leaders (including a Salvation Army officer, a churchwarden of an Anglican parish, and a Student Union official), who entered into dialogue with the candidates onstage to clarify any answers that were vague.

The political power of the alliance also explains the candidates' largely positive responses to the proposals. The number of people attending the churches, mosques, synagogues, and schools in the alliance was far in excess of the 62,538 votes by which the previous mayoral election had been won. As the Right Reverend Peter Hill (the Bishop of Barking) pointed out in his closing remarks, the six thousand people in the assembly hall participated in a network of relationships reaching hundreds of thousands of Londoners. This meant that the responses of the candidates would be transmitted through face-to-face conversations to a significant proportion of London's electorate—a number large enough to influence the outcome of the race.

The assembly was the most visible manifestation of London Citizens' power, but the strength of the alliance consists in the long-term nature of the relationships. The specific policy demands being made at the assembly grew out of much longer-term campaigns (for a living wage, affordable housing, and a better welcome for refugees). Because the campaigns and the alliance are both long-term, candidates knew that they would be held to the promises they made onstage.

As Tim Conder and Dan Rhodes remind us, "building power" is not an idea that churches find easy. (The same could be said of many other religious and civic organizations.) Writing from the context of the American church, they observe:

> "Power" in church contexts is usually a dirty word. It smacks of everything the church should not be: violent, competitive, duplicitous, and opportunist. It's no accident that good church folk bristle when the theme comes up and seek to expel it from the workings of the congregation. Power, in our society, is Machiavellian, the intrinsically corrupt but necessary tool of politicians and military generals in a complicated and fallen world—something that can at best be balanced in order for some semblance of peace to occur. Surely if Lord Acton was right, that "power corrupts and absolute power corrupts absolutely," then there's good reason to try to keep it out of the church.[5]

My own experience underscores the challenge of relieving religious leaders, in this case Christians, of their bias against wielding earthly power. In January 2017 all of the seminarians enrolled in the Church Divinity School of the Pacific (CDSP) in Berkley, California, were enrolled in the training of the Industrial Areas Foundation (IAF) as part of their formation. These Episcopalian candidates for ministry were trained in the core concepts of organizing alongside grassroots Christian, Jewish, and secular leaders. I also had the opportunity to participate in the program, along with a Jewish and a Muslim organizer from Citizens UK.

The seminarians took an hour each morning, before the IAF training, to theologically reflect on what they were being taught. By the third day of training, there was significant unease among the CDSP students around the positive valuation of "power" within the organizing movement. Does not power corrupt? Two things transformed the mood. The first was a session of theological reflection on the issue of power that offered a much more positive way of addressing the concept as a Christian. The second was a teaching session by Robert Hoo, the community organizer for Nevadans for the Common Good (NCG), the IAF affiliate for the city of Las Vegas. Hoo laid out the analysis of power dynamics in the city that the alliance had undertaken as part of a campaign for a change in the law that would make it easier for law enforcement agencies to tackle child sex trafficking. The forensic analysis of the strengths and the interests of the various economic and political players—casino owners, elected representatives, civil society organizations —brought home the reality of where power lies in this most hedonistic of cities.[6] To the trainees, faced with Hoo's account of the prevalence of child prostitution and the potential impact of NCG's proposal, there was only one possible answer to the question Do we want the power to turn our feelings of compassion and revulsion into practical change? The consensus was strongly in the affirmative.

The seminarians were recognizing a common truth within organizing: that those who need change the least are the ones most likely to problematize the issue of "building power." As Conder and Rhodes put it:

> In all honesty, those of us who have it like having it, and those of us who lack it either wish we had it and are trying to get it, or have simply given up. In our experience, it's often those who have quite a bit of power who tend not to want to talk about it or recognize it within the purified confines of the church. This is especially the case for upper middle-class white folks, who tend to enjoy the benefit of power more generally. Often what scares us about power is first and foremost the fact that, should we begin to recognize it, then we'd have to begin to recognize how much of it we have relative to others. Recognizing power means recognizing how frequently we get our way and how the existing structures benefit us more than others.[7]

THE USE OF TENSION

Alinsky was willing to use irreverence and humor in "actions" against politicians and business leaders. This use of tension was a direct consequence of his conviction that power is not given up without a struggle. Dramatic tactics might be used to apply moral or practical pressure to the target of such an action. For example, consider Alinsky's proposed "tie-up" of a bank:

> All banks want money and advertise for new . . . accounts. . . . [But] opening a savings account is more than a routine matter. First, you sit down with one of the multiple vice-presidents or employees and begin to fill out forms and respond to questions for at least thirty minutes.

If a thousand or more people all moved in, each with $5 or $10 to open up a savings account, the bank's floor functions would be paralyzed. . . . The bank is in a difficult position. . . . Its public image would be destroyed if some thousand would-be depositors were arrested or forcibly evicted from the premises.[8]

A more modest variant on this theme was used in the early stages of London Citizens Living Wage campaign to secure a meeting with Sir John Bond, the chairman of the Hong Kong and Shanghai Banking Corporation (HSBC). The bank had been chosen as one of the early targets of the Living Wage campaign as it was constructing its new global headquarters in Canary Wharf, a major development in East London that had been designed to regenerate the area. London Citizens' argument was that, if the regeneration was to benefit the poorest residents, it was crucial that the subcontracted workers who would clean, cater to, and guard the new building be paid a decent wage. Despite sending his office a number of letters from religious and civic leaders, London Citizens had been unable to secure a meeting with Sir John to discuss the poverty wages of those who cleaned the bank's new international headquarters in East London.

The nuns at St. Antony's Catholic Church in Forest Gate came up with an idea. The two thousand–strong congregation had an account with HSBC. Each Tuesday the nuns were accustomed to depositing in their local HSBC branch a large number of coins left each week by the many visitors who came into the church to light candles. The nuns decided to save up these coins for a few months, until they filled a small van. Just before Christmas, accompanied by a team of London Citizens leaders, they drove to HSBC's Oxford Street branch in the heart of the capital, near to BBC Broadcasting House. In full view of the national media, holding placards saying "Sir John Bond – Scrooge" and "Give HSBC a Living Wage for Christmas," the nuns tied up the branch completely by depositing their coins one by one. This exercise of tension had the desired result. Within an hour, Sir John had agreed to meet a team of London Citizens leaders. This was the beginning of the process (which included further occasions of high-profile tension, as well as more irenic negotiation) by which HSBC became one of London's first Living Wage employers.

As Khan and Goldsmith considered their responses to London Citizens' demands, they would have been aware that the alliance would use such tactics to hold them to *their* words. At the first Mayoral

Accountability Assembly, held in 2004, Ken Livingstone had promised to find a site for a Community Land Trust in East London. However, once in office, he proved reluctant to keep his word. In response, institutions of London Citizens formed a tented city on public land outside City Hall (the headquarters of the mayoralty) in July 2007. Each organization had its own tent and committed to filling it with members on a rotating basis. Throughout the day, the political action was interspersed with their regular rhythms of worship—with East London Mosque's delegation arranging Muslim prayer and St. Margaret's Catholic Parish in Canning Town offering an open-air Mass. This use of tension drew significant media coverage and led the mayor to keep his initial promise by identifying the site of a hospital already marked for closure in East London for the capital's first Community Land Trust. At the time of this writing, the first residents have now been given keys to their homes, sold to them at one-third of the market price, with a structure of ownership that ensures that the homes will remain affordable in perpetuity.

On the surface, this "action" had some obvious similarities to the Occupy LSX protests of 2011–12. But there are also striking differences. Whereas Occupy was a spontaneous movement of individuals and refused on principle to negotiate with the City of London about the demands it made, London Citizens' action was part of a long-term movement and a long-term negotiation with the mayor. When a community organizing alliance engages in public action, there is always a specific "target" (usually a named individual). Prior to the action, there is an analysis of the state of the relationship between the alliance and the individual, the interests of the individual, and the power of the alliance. In order for an action to go forward, the analysis must lead the alliance to conclude that the action to be taken will yield the desired outcome. That is why neither Alinsky nor contemporary organizers will ever use the term "protest" to describe the events in question. The term "action" is used in deliberate contrast: It is an exertion of collective power to move the campaign forward in a specific, measurable way.

FINANCIAL INDEPENDENCE

Alinsky understood that the financing of a community organizing movement would be critical. If the movement was to be genuinely independent, it needed to be funded by the people and institutions that were its members. London Citizens' 2016 assembly began with a "roll call" of its member institutions, including a recognition of the substantial membership dues paid by each one. In the early days of community organizing in the United Kingdom, there was concern that the roll call and the stress on membership dues were "too American." On each side of the Atlantic, however, this public drama demonstrates the diversity and numerical power of the alliance. At an assembly, the hall is not filled simply with interested individuals. They are organized citizens: The thousands in the hall represent many thousands more who gather each week in their churches, mosques, synagogues, and schools. Moreover, these citizens and their institutions are being publicly recognized. As one Roman Catholic priest said to me after an assembly: "My congregation have never before been applauded and welcomed by their neighbors in East London for being Catholics!"

The roll call is a public statement of the alliance's financial independence. In 2016, London Citizens' member organizations had not only turned out six thousand organized citizens; they had pledged over £250,000 to ensure that the alliance would be able to set its own priorities and act on its own concerns and interests.

Each IAF or Citizens UK alliance charges dues calculated on the basis of an institution's membership and revenue. These dues fund the recruitment and training of paid community organizers whose role is to identify and develop grassroots leaders in each member organization, help them to identify shared concerns, and then turn these problems into "winnable issues" on which their collective action can achieve practical change. In the end, it is only what Alinsky called "hard money"—funding from the institutions that constitute a community organizing alliance—that can truly guarantee that it is owned by its people.

As well as preserving the alliance's financial independence, the payment of membership dues discourages member institutions from developing a victim mentality. It is tempting for the institutions in poorer areas to become supplicants, using the stories of their neighborhoods' deprivation and poverty to gain funding from benefactors. The payment of membership dues is one of many ways in which community organizing moves such institutions from a mentality of dependency and victimhood to one in which they recognize their power to change things for the better.

This is often hard for others to understand. Jeffrey Stout describes the work of IAF in the *colonias* (shantytowns) of the Rio Grande as "one of the most impressive victories for grassroots democracy in the United States since the passage of the Civil Rights act in 1964." The alliance secured over $2 billion to bring water, wastewater, and other types of infrastructure to neighborhoods in unincorporated areas that lacked them.[9] As the campaign for better conditions gained traction, the national media became interested in the plight of the *colonia* dwellers and how they were being let down by the authorities. However, they were largely uninterested in the story of how those residents were organizing both people and money to change their conditions. As Stout puts it, the national press wanted to write stories that depicted passive victims and made their readers think "Ain't it awful":

> Depictions of this kind also render invisible the political agency, indeed the dignity, of the very people whose suffering is being portrayed. The nearly complete failure of social critics, as well as the mass media, to depict the democratic practices that have occasionally produced victories like the transformation of the *colonias* is a major source of desperation in our politics. One senses that something has gone terribly wrong. Pictures of the suffering poor confirm our fears and call forth our sympathy. And in that moment, we are imagining ourselves as either the savior of these people or, more likely, as unable to do anything meaningful to alleviate their condition.[10]

That community organizing not only involves action by the "suffering poor" but is a movement funded by their own money is a challenge to the stereotyped narrative of powerlessness and dependency.

SELF-INTEREST

While the large-scale public assembly represents community organizing at its most visible, the heart of the movement is the individual relational ("one-to-one") meeting. A paid community organizer will normally have around fifteen one-to-ones each week, and leaders of institutions in an alliance's membership are encouraged to have at least two or three. The purpose of these meetings is twofold: to build a "public relationship" (as distinct from a personal friendship) and to identify one another's "self-interest." In the language of community organizing, "self-interest" is not a synonym for "selfishness." Rather, the self-interest of an individual or organization is the interest that actually *animates* its work. As I explained in the previous chapter, citizens involved in community organizing are taught to identify their own and others' self-interest by asking:

- What relationships are central to this person's life?
- How does she spend her time and money, and why?
- What are the motivations for key decisions she has made?
- What institutions is she involved in, and why?

It is here that organizing has undergone the most striking evolution since Alinsky's death in 1972. Alinsky offered a purely pragmatic rationale for this focus on self-interest, and this inspired justified criticism of community organizing for promoting an excessively cynical account of human motivation. Under Chambers and his colleagues, a more nuanced account of self-interest developed, one that makes space for the role of values and vocation in human motivation. In fact, the questions at the heart of a "one-to-one" are entirely open. They make no judgment as to whether human beings in general are selfish or selfless. Rather, they initiate an honest exploration of what motivates the particular individuals who are in conversation.

The training community organizing alliances provide for their member institutions is devoted to developing the craft involved in conducting these individual relational meetings. Emphasis is placed on sensitivity, on probing without prying, and on creating a relationship that allows for public action rather than a personal friendship. Mutuality—the willingness to share the kinds of information about oneself that one is seeking to elicit about the other person—is also highly valued. Trainees in IAF and Citizens UK (whether paid organizers or grassroots leaders) are instructed to focus on the particular choices each person has made and the values and motivations that inspired her. Conversations about abstract values lacking an anchor in concrete actions are discouraged.

The rationale for engaging with the actual interests of the individuals and institutions of a community-organizing alliance is obvious: These are the practical things they care about and about which they are clearly motivated to act. However, there is also an ethical rationale for this focus. Organizing around citizens' self-interest honors their actual values and concerns by focusing on and respecting their lived moral commitments and the realities of their lives.

If we reflect on the four questions listed above, we will recognize that our self-interest is not static. In fact, mosques, churches, and synagogues all seek the transformation of their worshipers' self-interest by encouraging growth in their love of God and neighbor and by teaching that it is precisely in this opening of the heart that human beings find their ultimate fulfilment. For each of these religious organizations, true satisfaction is found when human beings begin to discern and pursue their God-given vocations. Indeed, it is only sin that prevents each person's self-interest and vocation from being completely aligned—and so, for congregations involved in community organizing, the one-to-one can become an important tool for vocational discernment. Michael Gecan argues that it can therefore be understood as a spiritual practice: "If the death of the spiritual life starts in 'talking past others' so frequently that you 'finally will no longer even notice it,' then the birth of the spiritual life starts in the individual, one-to-one meeting—in listening to the other person."[11]

The Reverend Vanessa Conant is team rector of the parish of Walthamstow in East London. She explains the role of one-to-ones and self-interest in the renewal of her congregation, illustrating the impact of discerning the interests of a congregation before moving to action:

> I have learned the value of one-to-one conversations in building congregations and that they are a vital part of work—meeting Roman Catholic priests who have congregations of thousands, yet who have hundreds and hundreds of one-to-ones has been inspiring and encouraging (and a bit of a challenge) when it sometimes feels as if the parish is too busy and demanding to fit them in.
>
> Seeing the difference that these one-to-ones has made has also been profoundly encouraging. They have helped me discover people's gifts, passions, and concerns. They have enabled me, out of that, to build new teams within the church and to develop new relationships. They have helped me to know the people in the congregation and to begin to think where we can grow. They have also encouraged me to think of new things—the organic nature of the process and the search for people's "self-interest" has meant that I can't control the conversation or the activity.

Daniel [the Citizens UK organizer in Waltham Forest] has been consistently supportive, encouraging, and inspiring. He has been thoughtful, insightful, and very compassionate. The church had been grappling with vision and direction. Now we have a clear direction for the year. I feel there is a more empowered congregation, leadership is being shared across the congregation, people are beginning to express interest in wider Citizens' actions, and some people who have never participated in anything are gradually being drawn in.

Just as participation in a religious congregation affects a worshiper's self-interest, the organizing process affects participants' relationships and motivations. The research our team conducted in inner-city London bears this out. Reflecting on his mosque's participation in a community-organizing campaign for single-sex hospital wards, Sarfraz Jeraj observed: "Our success in resolving this issue was only possible because we joined forces with other institutions. Working together made our cause more powerful, engendered more ideas about how to resolve the issue, allowed access to greater resources, and provided organization support to facilitate our goals. The experience helped to build trust and relationships with other communities and motivated us to support the work of other issues that affect Muslims and non-Muslims alike."[12]

The change in self-interest Jeraj describes is significant. The initial motivation to organize had been pragmatic: Relationships beyond the mosque were necessary in order to achieve something the mosque already wanted. However, the trust and solidarity built through common action motivated his mosque to campaign on other issues that affect people of all faiths and none.

Dilowar Khan is the director of East London Mosque and the London Muslim Centre. His reflection on the story of East London Mosque makes a similar point. Because organizing was done around an issue with which the mosque was immediately concerned (filing a planning application for an extension), relationships were built that led to action on a wider set of concerns. In the nineteen years since this campaign, East London Mosque has become deeply involved in the alliance—and has been at the heart of its campaigns for a living wage, "Local Jobs for Local People" in the London 2012 Olympics, and affordable housing. Here Khan explains how his institution has become deeply engaged in community organizing:

The East London Mosque and London Muslim Centre based in Whitechapel are founding members of London Citizens. The mosque celebrated its centennial anniversary in 2010 and is among the largest in the capital with over 5,000 worshippers regularly attending congregational prayers on Friday. The extension to the mosque, the London Muslim Centre, first opened on the 11th June 2004 after a campaign for the land. The center is home to a secondary school in the form of London East Academy, in addition to employment and training projects to facilitate community development.

One of our earliest campaigns and one of the most important in our experience as an institution involved in an alliance was the collective struggle we faced to acquire the land where our London Muslim Centre now stands. The need for more space and an extension became increasingly urgent as our communities kept growing. In 1998, an opportunity arose to acquire the land next to our mosque, the car park that was formerly a World War II bomb site. We discovered that a private property developer wanted to build high-rise private apartments on the space for commercial gain. Many of our non-Muslim colleagues through TELCO [the East London chapter of London Citizens] knew the importance of this space for the growth and development of our community and institution. They stood shoulder to shoulder with us and helped campaign to acquire the land through creative actions to show their support.

One Friday after Jummah prayers, we organized ourselves as a community with hundreds of people to form a giant human ring surrounding the mosque complex and the car park where we wanted the land. Through TELCO we had men, women, and children, of all faiths and none, show solidarity by standing with us to support our bid for the space, and the local media covered the story to put pressure on the property developer. We managed to persuade the property developer not to build in our community and to sell the property to the mosque. After we persuaded the developer, we still needed the planning permission from the local council to allow us to build on the land. Again through TELCO, we took action to ensure the council understood the full extent of the need for this space in our community. A team of leaders including a Catholic priest and religious sister chained themselves with a few of us from the mosque to the planning department at the council to highlight the significance of this issue.

The action was designed to get recognition and a relationship with council to discuss this issue. We managed to get a positive reaction from the council and permission to build our center. We could not have done this as effectively alone. The fact that diverse groups were organized as one community all saying *we need this land for our community* was the most radical persuasion you could have asked for. The actions showed the unity, strength, and power of public relationships in our communities. This is what relating to each other, trusting each other, and working with each other can achieve.[13]

This focus on self-interest is essential if community organizing is to be a movement *of* and not just *for* the poorest in society. Unless the priorities of an organizing alliance are set by the concerns of the member institutions, their members will neither feel ownership of the work nor participate in it to the full.

If an action is based on the leaders' estimation of what the community needs rather than the actual motivations of those experiencing injustice, most members of a congregation will tend not to get involved in the campaign. The action will therefore become no more than advocacy by one group on behalf of another. This isolated act will undermine the aim of building a genuinely populist movement. By contrast, when organizing begins with the immediate priorities of those who live with injustice, those members are engaged and gain, over time, the confidence to work on more strategic issues.

Community organizer Matthew Bolton offers another important motivation for the focus on self-interest. When one (generally more privileged) group is organizing on behalf of another, the former group may well fail to act in the best interests of the latter; in such a case, the more privileged group may be guilty of preferring the sensation of moral self-righteousness to the compromises that may be necessary to secure material progress. (This was an issue I identified in the previous chapter with respect to the Occupy LSX Camp and to left-wing populism more generally.) Bolton offers a telling anecdote from London Citizens' "Strangers into Citizens" campaign, which sought a one-off amnesty for undocumented migrants:

One Zimbabwean failed asylum seeker called Anthony, who is disabled through polio, made a compelling argument that we should include a condition that undocumented migrants gaining regularized status would not be able to claim benefits for a qualifying period of two years, as he thought it would make the issue more winnable. Generally, I found it was people who had "irregular" status themselves who were the most prepared to compromise access to any state support because they were so angry at being portrayed as scroungers and so desperate to come out of the shadows. But in the end it was largely the voices of people who were not in the situation themselves but for whom this idea of temporarily limiting benefits went against their principles that won out, and Anthony's suggestion was not included in our final campaign proposals.[14]

This dynamic has been a consistent experience during my own community-organizing work. Where people are actively involved in decisions that affect their own situations, they are motivated to achieve a more just solution and willing to be pragmatic. I was particularly struck by this during London Citizens' campaign to ensure that the 2012 Olympics (held in East London) benefited local people. Those resident in the boroughs where the Olympics were to be staged were keen to strike a deal that secured something meaningful to them—a living wage for those who worked on the site as it was prepared and during the Olympics; jobs fairs to ensure that local people had a good chance of employment on the site; and affordable housing in the Olympic Park afterward. They were less keen on running a campaign that made more ambitious demands but failed to secure a deal.

DEVELOPING LEADERS THROUGH ACTION

As well as placing those experiencing injustice at the heart of the struggle for change, Alinsky also sought to develop their capabilities through their common action. In community organizing, such action is at the heart of a wider pedagogical process. Through one-to-one conversations and subsequent meetings within and across institutions, the community-organizing alliance identifies common interests and problems affecting the lives of a diverse group of citizens. Members of those institutions then form research teams to identify the factors behind the problems, the steps that might be taken to address them, and who needs to take the steps (the targets of the actions). Taking into account the strength of the community-organizing alliance at the time in question, a realistic assessment is made of whether it has enough power to persuade the targets to take the actions in question.

To give a specific example, the London Living Wage Campaign emerged from the identification of the pressures on family and community life caused by the long hours many low-paid employees had to work. Whereas "long hours" and "low pay" are problems, the "London Living Wage" was a specific, measurable step to address it. The alliance took on the campaign for a living wage only at a point when it had sufficient power to persuade some of the key "targets" of its campaign (in the first instance, Sir John Bond and HSBC) to adopt a living wage as a policy.

As Ernesto Cortés explains, such victories are not only ends in themselves; they are lessons for public life. At each stage, he and his fellow organizers are identifying members of each institution who are capable of playing a role in a campaign that stretches them beyond their previous comfort zone but through which (with support and mentoring) they can grow in capability and confidence. "Action," as Cortés told me, "is to the organization what oxygen is to the human body. [It is] vital to our flourishing, but we don't live to breathe." It is through this pedagogy, he argues, that people come to a deeper and more expansive understanding of their interests. "As we begin to expand our interests, we become more and more concerned with others. Through action, we become interested in growing and developing as people in relationship with others. This emerges not by introspection but by engagement."[15]

Fr. Sean Connolly's ministry in East London exemplifies this slow, patient process of leadership development: engaging in one-to-one meetings, discerning self-interest, and developing the confidence of worshipers who had never previously acted in the public sphere. Fr. Sean arrived in Manor Park just before the Olympics. (His parish is in the London Borough of Newham, which contains the main Olympic Park.) That year one of the churches in his parish was celebrating its 150th anniversary. Because of the impending Olympics, the local council was unwilling to put up any new road signage. However, Fr. Sean's parishioners felt strongly that their church needed the same public recognition that many other local institutions had already received—and hence that this prohibition was arbitrary and unfair. These parishioners led a community organizing campaign called "We Don't Want a Miracle, We Just Want a Sign." The good-humored action they took (at a meeting of Newham Council) received significant local media coverage and led to an agreement by councilors (the "targets" of the action) to provide the sign. While it was a small victory, it was a very tangible one. Every time parishioners attended the church, they were reminded of what could be achieved by collective action. People who had never before had any experience of successful action to change the behavior of either government or corporate bodies began to envisage greater possibilities.

Five years later, the seemingly trivial victory around a sign led to successful campaigns against unjust evictions and in favor of new affordable housing in the area. By beginning with the motivations and concerns of parishioners, and moving only at the pace at which those motivations changed, Fr. Sean managed to achieve far more than if he had rushed into action on a more obviously strategic issue without first developing grassroots leaders.

The story told by Lucy Achola, a member of Fr. Sean's Catholic Parish of Manor Park, further illustrates this. Here she explains how she became a key leader in the housing campaign:

My name is Lucy Achola. I live in a three-bedroom house with my children, aged 11, 7, and 5, all in full-time education in the local area. We belong to St. Stephen's Parish Church, where we pray and feel part of the community.

The property I am living in belongs to Newham Council. It was leased to the housing association, ... my current landlord. The lease period has come to an end, and the housing association is returning the property to the rightful owner, Newham Council. When I contacted the council regarding the case, they responded by offering me a private rented property run by an estate agent. This is more expensive than their own council property, which is affordable in terms of rent.

I requested that the council let me continue to occupy the original property with my family due to the fact that the rent is affordable, we have formed a strong bond with the community where we live, and the children can go to school easily in terms of transport.

My request was rejected by the Newham Council Housing Team. They sent one of their staff to view the property while I was there. The man was very open to me. He told me that the reason why the council is not giving me the property is because they are afraid to lose the right to buy to me—they would rather keep the property and sell it in an open market, which will bring them good profit. I was left with no words, as this story clearly shows that the financial interest of the council comes before the essential needs of the community they serve, which includes offering affordable housing.

I really did not know what would happen to me, as the process of getting rid of me and my family from the house was still going ahead. It was so painful not to be listened to, to be forcefully removed from a place you call home, a place you can afford in term of rent. So, I joined the Housing Team at my church, St. Stephen's, because I was sick and tired about my housing situation. Our team had hundreds of one-to-ones in the parish. We heard lots of horror stories and invited our local councilor to a meeting to listen to them. I shared my story, along with Nadine, Simeon, and Chris. I was facing eviction from my home of seven years. I was so stressed about my family becoming homeless. Days after the councilor visited, I got a letter of eviction. I called on my councilor to intervene, and he did, using his power as the cabinet member for Housing. I am no longer facing eviction! I can now plan for the future, and I have peace of mind.

Later in this chapter, Lina's story of a Chicago mosque illustrates a related point. A focus on listening to members of the mosque was central to the development of new grassroots leaders so that the already busy group of veterans was not left with all of the work. Once again, this involved a patient process of engaging people in conversation and identifying common interests in order to widen the pool of members taking responsibility for the life of the institution.

The importance of patient, incremental development is borne out by testimony from community organizers in the United States seeking to engage low-paid staff in their workplaces. Those workers' experience of the slow erosion of rights and the victimization of anyone who challenges this process often leaves them skeptical of the claim that collective action will be in their interests. Low-paid workers are aware that community organizers have far less to lose from such action than they do. Successful action, therefore, needs to proceed incrementally: Small, winnable campaigns around immediate concerns (whether in the workplace, neighborhood, or church) can build confidence that change is possible and can also build the relationships that mean they are indeed safe when they take an action that challenges those who employ them.

This pedagogical aspect of organizing was also evident at the London Citizens' Assembly. In total, a hundred different people had specific roles on the stage, including participating in the roll call, giving testimony, chairing the event, acting as timekeepers, presenting London Citizens' demands to the candidates, and asking the candidates follow-up questions based on their responses. At the end of this assembly, as in the cases of all assemblies and actions held by a community organizing alliance, an evaluation was held. On this occasion, it involved around two hundred people—leaders of member institutions and community organizers as well as most of the hundred people who had played roles on stage. These evaluations always have a pedagogical function, as they identify which aspects of the craft of organizing were done well and which could be improved. For example, two important criteria for evaluation of any such event are whether new leaders were involved for the first time and which of the experienced leaders participating in the event had the opportunity to advance to a new stage in their participation in public life. At this particular assembly, a further question would be whether those leaders represented a genuine cross section of the alliance and of the wider body of Londoners who experience social injustice.

This constant focus on pedagogy and evaluation is crucial to keeping London Citizens rooted in the lives of the city's poorest residents.

ARTICULATING THE DISTINCTIVE MOTIVATIONS
FOR COMMON ACTION

In perhaps its greatest contrast with a liberal approach to politics, organizing allows participating communities to give distinct accounts of the reasons for acting on an issue. This act of *mutual witness* is a practical embodiment of negotiated pluralism. An alliance such as London Citizens allows each institution to draw on its distinctive conceptions of the good. The alliance acts on only the issues on which those conceptions overlap—and these diverse groups can therefore agree on common objectives.

Whereas Alinsky tended to instrumentalize these institutions, under the leadership of Chambers, IAF began to engage at greater depth with their values and mission. In our own day, congregations of faith remain the only places where people from a wide range of backgrounds come together to form community and to make sense of their lives in the light of a larger account of reality. The other institutions of civil society tend to have particular functions (e.g., schools and universities or charities promoting specific goals) or to serve a particular interest group (e.g., trade and student unions and resident associations). Despite the common image of religious congregations as divisive, they are in fact the places in UK society where people are most likely to meet others who are different from them.

The range of issues on which quite different religious and secular groups can reach a common purpose is surprisingly large. Such common action is capable of yielding substantial changes. As well as securing the first anti-usury laws in the United Kingdom for over 170 years and winning £500 million for low-paid workers through the Living Wage Campaign,[16] Citizens UK has helped to secure policy changes on the ending of child detention in the sanctuary process and on the resettlement of three thousand refugees from Syria in the United Kingdom.

Similarly, IAF lists among its "signature accomplishments" the securing of $2 billion of infrastructure for *colonia* dwellers in Texas and the lifting of more than eleven thousand people out of poverty-level jobs and into careers paying a living wage in Texas, Arizona, and Louisiana. When Texas IAF organizations took relational organizing principles into low-income neighborhoods and engaged parents and communities in the transformation of their schools, they created what became widely recognized as a successful strategy for school reform.

East Brooklyn Congregations, an IAF affiliate in New York City, pioneered the Nehemiah Housing strategy to replace hundreds of acres of blighted, abandoned housing with large-scale developments of new, high-quality housing that was affordable for ownership to low- and moderate-income residents of those communities. (Since 1983, over 4,500 Nehemiah Homes have been built in East New York, over 1,000 in the South Bronx, over 1,000 in Baltimore, and over 250 in Washington, DC.)

BUILD, the IAF Affiliate in Baltimore, conceived of and implemented the nation's (and the world's) first living wage ordinance; the living wage has since been implemented in more than two hundred communities around the world.

Finally, the Greater Boston Interfaith Organization, the IAF affiliate in Massachusetts, spearheaded the statewide coalition that pushed through Massachusetts's 2006 bipartisan universal health care law, signed by then-governor Mitt Romney. This groundbreaking legislation, which provided access to life-saving health coverage for 500,000 Massachusetts residents, became the template for the national Affordable Care Act.[17]

The process of organizing is pluralist in that it harnesses quite divergent conceptions of the good life. In terms of religious conceptions, it works as well in a Catholic parish as in a Jewish congregation. Jeffrey Stout's study of organizing in Southwest IAF offers a number of striking examples of the adaptability of the process to Catholic as well as to Baptist churches, including the parish of St. Joseph the Worker in McAllen, Texas, in the Rio Grande Valley. Its priest explains the work as follows: "You have to speak with a congregation and speak about principles of involvement," Father Alfonso said. "What is the tradition of our faith? What is the social doctrine of our faith? I tried to integrate that with the sense that it is part of our spiritual life. Spiritual life is what we do all of the time. It's what happens at school. It's what happens at work. It's what happens with family. They're all connected, so that we were very fortunate to have lots of church documents that support that kind of a teaching—the social doctrine of the church." Liturgy is at least as important to the spiritual dimension of politics as doctrine is, he said, because of its capacity to knit the parish together and to connect parishioners with the broader community. "It's a matter of helping people to be connected with one another."[18]

The story of organizing in the Congregation B'nai Jehoshua Beth Elohim illustrates the way organizing is rooted in the specific traditions and doctrines of each faith community. Community organizer Matt McDermott explains how organizing contributed to the renewal of this Illinois synagogue:

> Congregation B'nai Jehoshua Beth Elohim (BJBE) is a Reform Jewish congregation of approximately 850 families in Glenview, Illinois. In the middle of 2003, a new Rabbinic team arrived at BJBE—senior Rabbi Karyn Kedar and associate Rabbi John Linder. Rabbi Kedar quickly began to focus on a long-term strategy for congregational strength and growth. In September 2005, Rabbi Linder delivered a sermon during the Rosh Hashanah service focusing on the idea of building relationships within the congregation as a way to build community, identify new leadership, and engage in *tikkun olam*, the Jewish commandment to "repair the world."

Rabbi Linder's sermon planted the seeds of what BJBE would come to call Panim El Panim, which is Hebrew for "face to face." The name refers to Genesis 32, where Jacob wrestles with the divine in a dream. He is said to be "panim el panim" with God. The September sermon, however, did not lead to immediate action. Internal concerns about potential conflict or distraction from the capital campaign had to be navigated. Additionally, the social action leadership was busy that fall putting together a congregational response to Hurricane Katrina.

The Panim El Panim project began in earnest in January 2006 when 37 leaders from the congregation attended half-day training on relational one-to-one meetings. At the end of the training, several lay leaders asked their peers to take a list of ten names of fellow congregants. Each was asked to commit to doing at least five relational meetings and turn in simple report forms afterwards. By March, the team had completed 113 meetings. After Passover, in May, the emerging leadership team organized what they called a "celebration to action" assembly. More than 60 congregants attended and 15 leaders from neighboring United Power member institutions were guests. Three social action themes emerged from the initial one to ones: Healthcare, Education and Diversity/Tolerance.

During the summer, the leadership team identified leaders for two of the three themes and Health and Education Teams were formed. Soon after, a third team was formed to continue further one-to-one conversations. By the fall, the two new issue teams conducted ten house meetings, involving 100 leaders, to hone in on what health or education issues they might act on.

Already, even at this early stage, the results of this deepening work began to show: 35 BJBE leaders turned out to the United Power's countywide assembly in October 2006 with the governor. At a similar assembly a year earlier, just two attended. By April 2007, BJBE hosted a regional assembly of over 350 people on health care issues, delivering their local legislators and 95 people. Rabbi Linder, Lynn Wax, Judith Gethner, Julie Webb, the Taitel family, and other synagogue leaders played key roles in the assembly. Representatives from eight other congregations and a sister IAF organization, Lake County United, attended.

To date more than 220 relational meetings have taken place, dozens of house meetings [have been held], and nearly 50 people are regularly involved in the broader effort.[19]

Our research tested the depth and authenticity of this pluralism in the context of British organizing. Religious participants were very clear about the theological motivations for their action. As Dilowar Khan explains: "It is a requirement of my faith to be involved in the common good, and the work of TELCO reminds me of the Covenant of Virtue, where you uphold justice in society together with others. I like meeting people of other faiths and backgrounds and building a common understanding. Through this relationship building I can be of benefit to the community and also answer questions and remove any misunderstanding of Muslims and my faith."[20] A Roman Catholic priest and evangelical Anglican worshiper gave rather different accounts of their Christian motivation. "Being involved in organizing is one of the best ways of living my faith—I belong to a faith where everyone is welcome," the priest commented. "The Bible tells us to love God and to love your neighbor, but you can't do one without the other." The evangelical worshiper said, "My self-interest is that people would come to know Christ. That's it. I don't want to do that in a coercive way, I just want that desperately for more people, and for them to know the love of God, and that's that." He continued: "And so if part of expressing that is being with you and serving the poor, feeding kids, getting people homes, I'm like 'That sounds cool to me. Let's do that.'"

Interviewees were very clear that the relationships built by community organizing could be a space for a mutual witness in which they could be honest about differences of religion and belief—but not one in which it was appropriate to engage in debating the merits of incompatible doctrines (even if one's self-interest included the desire to bring people to one's own particular faith). "Citizens UK allows for people to not pretend ... there is this space where people don't have to [pretend]. . . . It allows you to build relationships across difference because you're being honest," one interviewee noted.

Another explained that TELCO works well "when it brings together the church or another institution to work with us where there is a common understanding that we work on issues of social justice for the common good of our communities, like the City Safe campaign in Shadwell. We have had meetings here at our mosque and centre and over at the church. It would break down all trust and relationships we have built if this access was used to openly preach and try and convert our congregations."

Many of those interviewed in our research in London felt that their faith motivations had been stifled or silenced in other contexts. A church leader described having become "conditioned to play faith down" in public contexts and cited the local manifestation of New Deal for Communities as an example of public activity in which "faith was almost sort of tolerated rather than anything else." In a similar vein, a Muslim community organizer explained that in his local area, "the youth programs are excellent examples of places where you try to be as secular as possible, and in that you miss out. . . . The reason why they're there trying to do a good thing is completely about their faith." Another organizer trainee described his experience in student politics in a similar way, saying: "During my time as an elected Student Union officer it was more or less implied that faith was restricted to the Christian Union groups and the societies, but when it came to meetings it was strictly political views."[21]

This resonates with other research. A Church Urban Fund survey found that 44 percent of more than a hundred faith representatives in Local Public Partnerships felt that the main partners were not open to discussing faith issues, while another academic came across similar themes in the voluntary sector, noting that "faith groups may also find it difficult to express religious values, beliefs, and principles in a more secularized policy context due to fear of sounding 'a bit weird.'"[22] As Adam Dinham observes, "The motivations of faith actors and those from government and public agencies may be very different," and "while these differences are unacknowledged, partners are destined to work in 'parallel languages.'"[23]

Nonreligious participants in Citizens UK do not seem to have been put off by the articulation of faith as a motivation for involvement. The following comment is typical: "I don't see an issue with faith and secular leaders coming together in the alliance. I think in many working-class areas faith organizations have always been a feature in deprived communities and often worked for change together, for example, in the 1860s and the history of the East End." Indeed, some said that being part of a Citizens UK alliance had changed their perspective: "I used to be a fairly aggressive atheist, I suppose, and thought there was no space for religion in the public square, and now I feel differently—I just think those faith institutions are engines of social capital, and in the end what they do is turn up, in numbers, and turning up in life is half the battle."

This is not to say that the process of sharing core motivations and building action around them is without its problems. Barclay's research identifies two key issues: insincerity and exclusivity. As he explains: "The first challenge, which is often encountered, is not that expressions of faith can be divisive, but rather that encouraging them can seem inauthentic or insincere. This is often the charge leveled in the American political context, where talk of religious motivation can be seen as a kind of routine that politicians need to go through to prove their suitability for public office."[24]

The charge of exclusivity was more often heard from secular interviewees, who sometimes felt that an open discussion of core motivations resulted in the prioritizing of some types of inspiration over others. One interviewee said that Citizens UK "obviously gets a lot of stick for being too faith-y, particularly on the left," and another explained that "a lot of people that I've brought to London Citizens events who are from the left or trade unions or both then find the religious side of it slightly strange."

One nonreligious interviewee also wondered whether more could be done to explore secular traditions in public meetings, asking: "What are the civic traditions that have some really articulate speakers that could be read at the same time [as from religious texts]?"

Such worries about exclusivity may flow from the mistaken conviction (prevalent more on the left than on the right in Britain) that a public discourse devoid of religious reasoning would be unproblematically "neutral." There was no suggestion in any of the interviews that nonreligious people feel *unwelcome* at Citizens UK events. Rather, there is a distaste for the "strangeness" of "faith-y" language. As the previous quotation indicates, nonreligious people are unused to articulating their own moral and ethical sources in a plural space. The move from secular liberalism to negotiated pluralism also gives them an opportunity for a more articulate witness to their values. Organizing alliances may need to be thoughtful and proactive in encouraging such secular witness.

STRENGTHENING INSTITUTIONS

Alongside the extensive literature on secularization stands a growing body of research on the atomized nature of modern Western societies.[25] Two features make organizing particularly attractive to religious institutions. First, as we have just seen, it respects the deep diversity of their interests and values in a way that many other allegedly "inclusive" practices do not. Second, organizing does not simply deplete a fixed stock of staff and volunteer time; the practice, when done well, strengthens the institutions that become members, an achievement that serves the interests of the wider alliance as well as the individual congregations. The national leadership of IAF has identified this as one of its most pressing concerns. As Jeffrey Stout explains:

> The situation of the Have-Nots today, according to [Ernie] Cortés [the co-director of IAF], is one in which many of the institutions that once buffered citizens from the market are themselves either falling apart or fighting for their lives. . . . More and more of the organizer's work must therefore, according to Cortés, be devoted to "reweaving the social fabric," which is largely a matter of strengthening the relational life of institutions that have chosen to join, or might be persuaded to join, a citizens' organization. "To rebuild our society," Cortés says, "we must rebuild our civic and political institutions. Under conditions of social fragmentation, it is a daunting challenge.[26]

The story of New Hope Lutheran Church illustrates the potential of organizing for strengthening institutions as well as building relationships between diverse organizations. New Hope is a black Lutheran congregation in the Queens borough of New York City. Tim Conder and Dan Rhodes explain how community organizing has strengthened the church:

> Like so many contemporary congregations, New Hope was a struggling church formed from the merger of three failing congregations, and it had recently called a new minister. Having looked to the local community organization to help address an infestation of drug dealing on and around the church premises, with [the] help [of Gerald Taylor, the local IAF organizer] they'd been able to win a quick and decisive victory by garnering the help of the local police. This victory boosted their ego a bit and established some recognition in the community.
> Shortly afterward, however, they were mired in a stewardship campaign that was failing miserably, with very few of the members actually signing pledges. Again, the minister turned to Gerald for

some help. At that point, Gerald asked the pastor and church leadership if they'd asked the people what their priorities for the community were. Essentially, he wanted to know, had they engaged in listening to the needs, desires, cries, and priorities of the members? Brushing this question off, the pastor and leadership relayed that they already knew what the priorities of the community were, so there was no need to engage in this activity. Always one for a good challenge (and quick to see a savvy opportunity, we would add), Gerald suggested that they "make a deal." He proposed that they let him run a series of house meetings to elicit the priorities of the community and then draw up their capital campaign based on those concerns. Then, if any of the priorities matched their pre-named priorities or they didn't make budget, he'd cut their dues to IAF in half. On the other hand, if a new set of priorities emerged and they made budget, then they would agree to double their dues to the organization.

You can likely guess the conclusion. At the end of the series of house meetings, not a single priority pre-identified by the church leadership made the list. Even more, when the church redesigned the campaign around the priorities that emerged from the house meetings (getting a new heating system and new carpet for the sanctuary, establishing some Bible study training), 147 out of 150 members made pledges, allowing them to raise their entire budget—with a surplus, to boot. Of course, Gerald called in his side of the deal, and this congregation went on to become the fastest-growing and largest black Lutheran church in New York City: New Hope Lutheran Church.[27]

Over the past ten years, the Centre for Theology and Community (CTC) has been working with churches involved in London Citizens. Across very different denominations and traditions, we have identified seven hallmarks of an organized church, ways in which the practices of organizing can strengthen the lives of local congregations. In identifying these seven hallmarks we were helped by work done in the United States by Pastor John Heinemeier (a Lutheran leader in IAF)[28] and by conversations with Sister Judy Donovan and Sister Pearl Caesar, who are involved in congregational development in IAF in the southern and western United States. What follows is a summary of the "hallmarks of an organized church" and their implications for a wider set of religious and civic institutions:

- **Integrating theology, spirituality, and action**. In many congregations, community engagement and social action feel like "foreign affairs"—the passion of a small number of church members but not part of the institution's "core business." If social action is to move from the periphery to the core of a church's life, worship and teaching will need to express the connection between the two.
- **Developing a relational culture**. Many institutions consider themselves to be friendly. However, it is usually the case that some people are made to feel more welcome than others. This is not always intentional. If an institution is dominated by one or two cultures, age groups, and/or social classes, it is easy for those who are different to be (more or less subtly) marginalized. A relational culture involves the intentional cultivation of relationships across difference. This could mean organizing a number of "one-to-one campaigns" each year in which members will schedule one-to-one meetings with people they know less well. Training would be offered to members in how to conduct such meetings so that the meetings will be deep without being intrusive and will be genuinely mutual conversations. As well as one-to-one meetings, the institution will regularly arrange "house meetings" at which people can listen to each other and move from conversation into practical action.
- **Constantly reorganizing to renew the focus on people**. In a maxim beloved by community organizers on both sides of the Atlantic, "All organizing is disorganizing and reorganizing." An institution that has taken community organizing to its heart is in a perpetual process of being transformed. Relationships require constant care and maintenance, and churches always need to guard against the tendency to become bogged down in bureaucratic processes or dominated by unrepresentative cliques. An organized institution will constantly be evaluating whether its meetings allow every voice to be heard; whether people from different cultures, age groups, and classes are involved in leadership; and whether its activities genuinely reflect the concerns and values of the whole membership—as well as whether they are accessible to those on its fringes.
- **Developing leaders through public action at a sustainable pace**. Developing leaders is as important as any other institutional goal. For example, the process of preparing for, executing, and evaluating

a church council or trade union meeting is as important as any-thing the meeting will decide. Community organizing encourages congregations to see every part of their lives as an opportunity to develop new leaders. Rather than a small band of people doing everything, an organized institution will have a growing number of members clearly gaining confidence about their leadership ca-pabilities, both in its internal life and in the public arena. Activities within the institution, and community organizing campaigns be-yond its walls, will be selected with the development of new leaders as an explicit goal. Precisely because the institution is focused on developing new leaders, it will not overwork any of its leaders but will support their private as well as their public commitments. This will express its focus on people, not projects: What happens to each person is more important than getting this or that done.

- **Sharing power and responsibility.** If an institution is serious about developing a broad team of leaders who take responsibility for its life, it will have to be patient. New activities will develop only at the pace that trained members own them. They won't be developed on the whim of the paid officers. When power is shared in this way, responsibility and ownership are also shared. This cre-ates a resilient team of leaders that will be less vulnerable to staff turnover. An organized institution understands that holding each other (and others) accountable is a basic form of respect. Both within the organization and in public life, members will be expec-tantly and appropriately agitational, prompting one another to ex-pand their horizons, accountability, and growth. As one American pastor put it, community organizing "understands agitation to be a form of love."

- **Having an instinctive readiness to work with others.** Institutions involved in organizing understand the need for collective power in order to realize the common good, and so see the need to build relationships across deep difference. Their members are willing to be acted upon by those beyond its walls, as well as to act upon them.

- **Telling and embodying the story of its faith.** Both telling and hearing one another's stories, within the congregation and in the public arena, are at the heart of the congregational culture. That is, a congregation seeks whenever possible to connect its stories with the stories of their scriptures.

While our research has focused on congregations of faith, there are parallel programs of institutional development in schools and trade unions in the IAF. All but the first and last of the hallmarks listed above are equally applicable to unions and nonreligious schools. Independent research on IAF's "Alliance Schools" program of institutional development (piloted in Texas and replicated by other chapters in the West and Southwest IAF) shows that it has had a positive impact on student attainment, parental engagement, and professional culture.[29]

As the stories in this chapter indicate, religious congregations come to organizing with different convictions and needs and so will contextualize these hallmarks in different ways. For example, for most Lutheran, Methodist, and Anglican/Episcopal churches, as well as for many synagogues and trade unions, increasing attendance and/or membership is a priority, whereas in many mosques, Baptist and Pentecostal churches, and Roman Catholic parishes, the challenge is developing relationships and grassroots leadership so that the already large attendance will lead to deeper engagement.

Lina Jamoul's story of organizing in a Chicago mosque underscores this latter challenge. Lina has worked as a community organizer on both sides of the Atlantic. Here she reflects on how a deeper engagement with the self-interest of members of a Chicago mosque was essential to their development as leaders:

The Mosque Foundation, which some say is the largest mosque in the Midwest, is in the middle of an old industrial area in Chicago's southwest suburb of Bridgeview. For the last ten years, the Mosque Foundation has played a central role in United Power for Action and Justice. One of my jobs as an organizer with United Power has been to be more deliberate about developing and training local leaders in the Mosque Foundation to strengthen the mosque itself.

Through initial individual meetings with over 60 leaders from the Mosque Foundation, an idea began to emerge for a local campaign. Veteran leaders from the mosque, who had been involved with United Power on wider-scale issues like healthcare and immigration reform, wanted to expose more of the mosque's members to that kind of public experience.

Our starting point had to be not a specific issue but a commitment to engage, relate to, and hear the stories of hundreds of members of the mosque. Some leaders wanted to jump straight to the specific issue we would work on. A number of leaders, including the influential and dynamic Imam, Sheik Jamal Said, said, "We already know our community well and have a sense of what our issues are." In many ways, they were right. It's not that leaders don't already listen or relate to their people. They wouldn't be leaders if they didn't. But all too often, even the most sensitive local leaders begin to assume that they know all there is to know about their members' needs. Even they need to take some time out from their task-oriented routines to do a new round of individual meetings, to ask basic questions of people they see on a regular basis, and to relate more intentionally to their followers. When they do, they often are surprised by what they learn.

Out of the 60 leaders we initially met with, the most talented ones and those who had the highest interest were identified and approached again with the idea of hosting a "listening evening" at the Mosque Foundation, run by leaders who would be trained by United Power. Many of the leaders we built this action around knew that they needed training to listen, to ask the right questions, and to agitate. Fourteen leaders were trained to run the listening session. They coined the phrase "town hall meeting" for the event, arranged the logistics, and worked on the turnout.

The town hall meeting itself was actually not one big meeting, but about ten smaller meetings with 150 people, each with the same agenda: to engage the people who came out in a conversation about what was important to them; about what things they were most worried about in their community; about what changes they wanted to see happen; and about how they saw themselves getting more involved in the problems they were concerned about.

The action was partly about training leaders in the Mosque Foundation how to be deliberate about these conversations. Many of the best leaders have this ability almost naturally; they ask the best questions because they listen well. We weren't teaching leaders anything they didn't already know. We were just getting them to be more intentional about creating a space inside the mosque for these kinds of public conversations to take place—not as an adjunct to a larger meeting, but as the meeting itself. The conversations weren't part of a larger agenda. For that evening, they were the agenda.[30]

CONCLUSION

This chapter has described the key features of the practice of community organizing and explained how they seek to build a movement that is both inclusive and populist, rooted in the lives and institutions of the poorest residents and focused on forming them as active citizens, strengthening their institutions, and building new relationships between them. As Ernesto Cortés explains, these processes are mutually reinforcing. It is largely through acting on the interests they share with their neighbors that citizens are created. Their institutions both shape them for this action, and are revitalized by it.[31]

My account thus far raises a number of questions, some more theoretical and some more practical. In chapter 3 I will situate my critique of liberalism within the wider academic debate on the subject. In chapter 4 I will address a number of more specific questions and concerns about the organizing method: What if the power built by organizing was put to destructive purposes? How much power in the alliance do the paid community organizers have? How does the description I have offered square with the highly cynical remarks Alinsky makes about morality and "self-interest"?

Perhaps the most serious question about organizing concerns its impact: If IAF has been organizing since the 1930s, why are we currently in such a crisis? To answer that question, we must first explore the corrosive effect secularizing liberalism has had on our political culture, for this, I will argue, is where our present crisis has its ultimate origins.

CHAPTER 3

Engaging the Theoretical Debate I

A Critique of Liberalism

Much of the disagreement in Anglo-American politics could, until recently, have been traced to the conflicting political philosophies of John Rawls and Robert Nozick. Rawls argues for an active state that redistributes wealth and ensures fairness for all, whereas Nozick argues for a "night-watchman" state that interferes as little as possible with the process of just acquisition and transfer of property by individuals in a laissez-faire economy. It is not a coincidence that both Rawls and Nozick describe their positions as forms of liberalism. The premise of both of their political philosophies (implicit in that of Nozick and made explicit in that of Rawls) is what I have termed secularizing liberalism—the belief that the reasons we offer in political discourse ought to be ones that will be compelling to citizens regardless of their *convictions* and therefore regardless of their substantive conceptions of the good. As we have seen, community organizing rejects this premise and encourages the diverse *convictions* of its member institutions to be articulated in political discourse.

In this chapter I will offer a twofold defense of this pluralist approach against the secularizing liberalism of Rawls and Nozick. I will begin with an examination of Rawls's case for such a liberalism and will argue that his self-image of neutrality is mistaken. While secularizing liberalism claims to be fair to different religious and metaphysical *convictions*, it turns out to favor the *convictions* of a particular kind of citizen (of whom, unsurprisingly, Rawls is a prime example). I will then go on to offer an even more fundamental objection to his approach—arguing that the conception of the will that underlies it is incoherent. Not only is it *unfair* to exclude substantive conceptions of the good from political discourse; without such conceptions we lose a handle on what it is for human beings to exercise liberty at all. I will argue that secularizing liberalism unwittingly undermines liberty both in theory and (increasingly) in practice.

RAWLS'S DEFENSE OF SECULARIZING LIBERALISM

John Rawls offers a detailed case for the exclusion of religious arguments from public reasoning, set out most clearly in his 1993 work *Political Liberalism*. He is willing to acknowledge that the effect of this exclusion may be to disadvantage religious worldviews, but argues that religious believers still have reason to accept such a settlement.

Rawls begins his argument by advocating the "priority of the right over the good." Different individuals and communities have different conceptions of the good life, and it is impossible to reach a rational resolution of their disagreements. Therefore, Rawls argues, there is a need for a fair basis for cooperation between these individuals and communities. It is this domain—of the "right" cooperation within a framework of law—that he terms "political."

Rawls calls this political framework one of "justice as fairness." He explains it as follows: "The fundamental organizing idea of justice as fairness, within which the other basic ideas are systematically connected, is that of society as a fair system of cooperation over time, from one generation to the next." Rawls is inviting citizens to step out from their "particular point of view" when they consider what would be a fair way for people of different worldviews to cooperate. We all have a personal morality, and we may be members of specific associations and accept particular religious or philosophical doctrines. But when we consider how to cooperate across diversity, these points of view "are not, in general, to be introduced into the political discussion of constitutional essentials and basic questions of justice."[1]

"Justice as fairness" is not intended to be a substantive account of what our lives are *for*; rather, it offers a process for living together and co-operating, given that we have such *different* accounts of what life is for.

What would it mean to step outside our particular points of view in order to establish a fair basis for cooperation? Rawls invites us to enter into a thought experiment, to imagine ourselves in what he calls the "Original Position," standing behind a "veil of ignorance" where we do not know what substantive views we will have. From imagining the judg-ments we would make in the Original Position, we can establish what would count as fair treatment, both in the distribution of resources and in the framework within which diverse groups live together.[2] He writes: "The idea of social cooperation requires an idea of each participant's ra-tional advantage, or good. This idea of good specifies what those who are engaged in cooperation, whether individuals, families or associations, or even the governments of peoples, are trying to achieve, when the scheme is viewed from their own standpoint."[3]

This paragraph is revealing: Rawls's political liberalism is in fact a product of a very particular understanding of the nature of moral judg-ments. "Rational advantage" and "good" are elided in Rawls's account. It is a substantive, controversial claim that what is good for all persons is to pursue their "rational advantage." (Moreover, as I will argue below, it is not clear that we can specify what someone's "rational advantage" is without already having a conception of what is good for them.)

From most ethical points of view, I have no reason to believe that my own advantage counts for more than anyone else's. Rawls is a moral con-structivist,[4] but those with a more realist approach to moral goodness (of which there are a wide and nuanced variety)[5] have no reason to accept his argument.[6] Precisely because, on such realist accounts, such conceptions of the good are beliefs about *what is true* rather than simply personal in-terests and preferences, it is not appropriate to use the same process to resolve differences in our interests as we use to resolve differences in our conception of the good life.

Far from being a neutral mediator between the diverse *convictions* in a pluralist society, Rawls's argument is compelling only for those who already share a significant part of his moral ontology. If you are a moral constructivist—and do not believe there is anything objective for different substantive conceptions of the good life to be "right" or "wrong" about—it makes sense to think that fair cooperation will need to be *neutral* with respect to those conceptions. By contrast, if you think those conceptions both are rationally defensible and relate to something objective, you will want a political process in which citizens are able to deliberate (among other things) about the nature of the good life.

Many moral realists—among them the overwhelming majority of Christians—think that truth claims about the good life are open to rational defense. They regard them, indeed, as open to the same kind of rational scrutiny as are the arguments that Rawls is making. Consequently, they will not have any reason to stand back from those commitments in the Original Position.

Rawls would reply that, however "publicly accessible" you may take arguments for your conception of the good to be, they are not in fact shared by all citizens. Therefore, we need some kind of process for discerning a fair basis for cooperation among those who continue to disagree with us, even after we have argued for our substantive conception of the good life.

This rejoinder, though, is question-begging. For it seeks to problematize ongoing disagreements about the *good* (even though publicly accessible reasons are being advanced for the rival substantive conceptions of the good life) while advancing a conception of the *right* that rests on premises (most notably, moral constructivism) that many citizens reject.

As Chantal Mouffe observes, liberalism's self-image of neutrality not only is false. It also reinforces the interests of particular social and economic groups: "Liberal theorists envisage the field of politics as a neutral terrain in which different groups compete to occupy the positions of power, their objective being to dislodge others in order to occupy their place, without putting into question the dominant hegemony and profoundly transforming the relations of power. It is simply a competition among elites."[7] In rejecting a pluralistic, agonistic vision of politics, liberalism has generated the antagonisms that now fuel the divisive and false populisms at the heart of today's democratic crisis.

THE NEED FOR METAPHYSICS

Rawls's arguments proceed in a historical vacuum. This reflects his conception of the nature of political reasoning: It should offer arguments accessible to all rational agents, irrespective of their social or temporal location.

In *Inventing the Individual: The Origins of Western Liberalism*, Larry Siedentop reminds his readers that the conceptions of the human individual, and also of a state that guarantees liberty and acknowledges equality before the law, have emerged in a historical process.[8] He argues that this is a process in which a much less egalitarian conception of human nature (enshrined in the ordering of families and cities in Greek and Roman culture) is overthrown by the "social revolution" caused by the spread of the Christian Gospel.[9] His contention is that secularizing liberalism is seeking to hold on to the fruits of this historical process without reflecting on the tree that bore them.

Siedentop shows that in their historical forgetfulness, such expressions of liberalism are indeed in danger of cutting off the very branch on which they are sitting. Liberty and equality before the law are values that necessarily emerge from a wider account of the human person and the place of that person in the universe.

This argument of Siedentop can be accepted while rejecting altogether his positive assessment of the underlying philosophy of liberalism. While he is right to criticize liberalism for its historical forgetfulness, he is wrong to suggest that this is its only serious flaw.

Siedentop's positive assessment of liberalism relies on a theological argument. He narrates a progressive unfolding of the implications of the Gospel, which he believes reach their fulfillment in the secular, liberal state. Yet this involves a highly selective misreading of the teaching of the early Christians, and in doing so theologically over-emphasizes the notion of the moral agency of the individual as opposed to participation in Christ and in the corporate Body that is the Church. At the same time, Siedentop's reading of Paul as a simple egalitarian underplays the social revolution in Paul's writings, which (like the Gospels) are written from the vantage point of the poorest *as opposed to* the aristocratic elite.[10]

Moreover, Siedentop understands the embrace of voluntarism and nominalism by William of Ockham to be part of the progressive evolution of liberalism, whereas I will argue that it is rather a dangerous and ultimately self-subverting error. A great deal hangs on this point: as John Milbank and Adrian Pabst observe, the insistence by voluntarists such as Ockham that the divine will—and then, by inference, the wills of divinely created human beings—is the "primary determinant of reality" and has shaped "much of modern political thought all the way to Rawls."[11]

The voluntarists regarded God's will as "unconstrained by pre-established rational norms." In their view, the divine will is free to choose entirely as it pleases, and any qualification of this is understood as a *constraint*. They carry over this account of free willing—as an absence of constraint—to their understanding of the human will.

Such an understanding of the human will is self-subverting. For, as Warren Quinn has shown, when choices have *no* constraints at all, they do not thereby become freer. Unless choices are oriented toward some conception of the good, they cease to be describable as intelligible, rational choices at all.[12]

Quinn's argument is that we can come to see something as an action rather than a mere compulsion only if we see it as attempting to realize something we can recognize (or at least comprehend being recognized) as a genuine good. Therefore, far from acting as a *constraint* on human freedom, a substantive conception of the good—of that which the will seeks as "desirable" in a sense that is not constituted by the mere act of willing—is essential if human action is to be genuinely free. As Milbank and Pabst express the point, voluntarism reduces human agency initially to "will" and then to mere "drives." Shorn of an account of participation in an objective goodness, the action of the will becomes a meaningless end in itself. Voluntarism leads to a "nihilistic" liberalism.[13]

THE EDUCATION OF DESIRE

This detachment of "liberty" from any substantive conception of goodness, and from the intermediate institutions and practices that help citizens to educate their desires, has generated many of the current failings of liberalism. Its corrosive impact on values is not a flaw but an intrinsic feature of a theory that sets out to detach the idea of free choice from accounts of objective goodness. In Patrick Deneen's words, voluntarism is "the first revolution, and most basic aspect of liberalism," leading to its rejection of "the ancient conception of liberty as the learned capacity of human beings to conquer the slavish pursuit of base and hedonistic desires."[14]

Alexis de Tocqueville recognized that the form of democracy he saw emerging in the United States would be healthy only if there were sources for the formation of desire that stood distinct from the homogenizing force of either state or market. As Deneen observes: "The more individuated the polity, the more likely that a mass of individuals would inevitably turn to the state in times of need. This observation (echoing one originally made by Tocqueville), suggests that individualism is not the alternative to statism but its very cause. Tocqueville, unlike so many of his current conservative and progressive readers, understood that individualism was not the solution to the problem of an increasingly centralized state but the source of its increasing power."[15]

Tocqueville ascribed the health of democracy that he encountered in New England to the Puritan ethos they had taken across the Atlantic. They were not creating a society *ex nihilo* but drawing on "wonderful elements of order and morality" that they had brought with them.[16] His fear was that the very practices of democracy would erode this ethos. As Sheldon Wolin explains, Tocqueville mourned the passing of the premodern vision of aristocracy as "an elite distinguished by public virtues" rather than simply "defined by interests" in the absence of an aristocracy.[17] In America's new democracy, political participants no longer understood their participation in public life in terms of lofty (if sometimes hypocritical) ideals but in predominantly materialistic terms: "[If] instead of a brilliant society, it is enough for you to live in a prosperous one, and . . . if for you the main object of government is not to achieve the greatest power or glory possible but to provide for each individual the greatest well-being, then you should equalize conditions and establish a democratic government."[18]

A CHRISTIAN POPULISM?

Tocqueville expresses a dilemma for the politics of his day: a choice between an *aristocratic* conception of politics that is elitist and focused on "public virtues" and "brilliance" and a *democratic* conception that is less noble and more "materialistic"—aiming at the contentment of the "masses" rather than the education of their desires. Neither branch of this dilemma is attractive. (For example, by aligning Christianity with voluntarism, egalitarianism, and mass democracy, Siedentop seems to embrace the latter choice for our own day—and then to be surprised by its consequences for public virtue.)

The Christian vision provides one way to resolve this dilemma. It refuses the choice between the excellence of a powerful aristocracy and the uncritical embrace of existing desires. Rather it offers a vision of ethical and spiritual renewal that begins within the poorest communities instead of one that is imposed by a social and political elite.

It was such a vision that fired the early Church. In the centuries that followed, this vision had a profound impact on the Roman Empire. Peter Brown, a leading historian of late antiquity, argues that the witness of the early Church represents a form of "Christian populism which flouted the cultures of the governing classes and claimed to have brought, instead, simple words, endowed with divine authority, to the masses of the Empire." It must be acknowledged, however, that this early vision proved hard to sustain. Whereas the New Testament portrays Jesus and the first Apostles as from lower social classes, Brown suggests that by the fourth and fifth century the original populism of Christianity was being hollowed out; while the narrative remained one of the dignity of the humblest subjects in the Empire, those proclaiming the message were now in fact "highly educated men" securing power for themselves through their relationship with the poorest rather than being participants in a genuine movement of the poorest in Roman society.[19]

In casting a vision of an authentic populism for our own times, Pope Francis is engaging in an act of *ressourcement*, resourcing contemporary debates by retrieving insights of the past. In doing so, he is recalling the Church to the witness of Scripture and the earliest Christians. This charts a path beyond a self-subverting liberalism to the education of desire that is essential if liberty is to be sustained.

As Ernesto Cortés explains, community organizing is built on precisely the institutions that make this education of desire possible—institutions that engage ordinary citizens in the tending of public life and are built around substantive conceptions of the good. Secularizing liberalism has contributed to the weakening of these institutions, and their renewal is essential to the building of a healthy democratic culture:

> It is not a constitution that makes a democracy, but the habits and practices of empathy, relationality, deliberation, negotiation, confrontation, argument, and ultimately compromise. This is the stuff of democracies. To a surprising degree, a plutocracy has emerged in our culture: one in which certain groups of people can manipulate the system to serve their interests and exempt themselves from normal requirements and restraints. This is reflected in the fact that both major

political parties are focused on the wealthiest 20 percent of families. . . . Notwithstanding the language of our Constitution and our laws, this cultural shift suggests an emerging caste system in the United States. The only way to curb such a shift is to rebuild the democratic institutions that develop in people their capacity to engage one another in the kind of reflection, relationships, and deliberations that are requisite for the functioning of a decent society.[20]

CHAPTER 4

Community Organizing

Six Challenges

In a column she wrote in September 2017 titled "Obama: Lucifer Is My Homeboy," Ann Coulter claimed:

> Alinsky is sort of the George Washington of "community organizers." He tried to hire Hillary to work for him right out of Wellesley. A generation later, those who had trained with Alinsky did hire Obama as a community organizer. . . .
>
> In the dedication in the first edition of Alinsky's seminal book, "Rules for Radicals," Alinsky wrote: "Lest we forget at least an over-the-shoulder acknowledgment to the very first radical: From all our legends, mythology and history (and who is to know where mythology leaves off and history begins—or which is which), the first radical known to man who rebelled against the establishment and did it so effectively that he at least won his own kingdom—Lucifer." I suppose it could have been worse. He could have dedicated his book to George Soros.[1]

The candidacy of Barack Obama led to an unprecedented focus on community organizing in US national politics. Coulter's article is one of the more lurid attacks on the practice, but a wider range of commentators expressed concern about Alinsky's teaching, along with fears that the infamous "Lucifer" dedication was symptomatic of a divisive and amoral approach to politics.

Having offered a theoretical defense of the pluralism at the heart of community organizing, in this chapter I will consider six more practical objections to organizing. The first three concern the *desirability* of Alinsky's approach:

- Is populism inherently dangerous?
- Is the focus of organizing on "self-interest" too cynical?
- Does organizing provide a platform for regressive groups?

The next three relate to the *effectiveness* of organizing. The experience of the Obama presidency gives the first of these a particular edge.

- If community organizing embodies an antidote to our current political woes, how did those woes intensify in the eight years in which an IAF-trained organizer was in the White House?
- Does organizing practice what it preaches?
- Does organizing embody a genuine pluralism?

IS POPULISM INHERENTLY DANGEROUS?

Like the word "power," "populism" promotes a mixture of reactions. As I have argued, community organizing is an unashamedly populist project. Critics worry that there is grave danger in building a mass movement of leaders trained to identify "targets" and run "actions" on them. Things may start benignly, with the movement fighting for a living wage and a welcome for refugees. The fear is that something is being built with the potential to be hijacked for more divisive and dangerous purposes.

As we saw in chapter 1, Luke Bretherton draws a helpful distinction between its "political" and "antipolitical" forms. Political populism, he writes, aims to "reinstate plurality and inhibit totalizing monopolies (whether of the state or market) through common action and deliberation premised on personal participation in and responsibility for tending public life."[2] He goes on to argue that the contemporary institution-based organizing of IAF and Citizens UK are forms of political populism, with an "emphasis on existing traditions and institutions" that distinguishes them from the liberal political theories that "view tradition with suspicion."

The institutions of civil society provide the space within which citizens can learn the vital democratic habits of negotiation and compromise through a range of different kinds of voluntary action. A healthy democracy cannot be sustained by statute: It requires these habits of good citizenship to be maintained. The plethora of grassroots institutions in civil society—such as religious congregations, tenants' associations, schools (and their parent-teacher organizations), rotary clubs, and trade unions—have a crucial role to play in this democratic pedagogy. In doing so they create an important bulwark against the power of any individual demagogue.

But the inclusive populism practiced by community organizers has an additional distinctive feature that offers a second level of defense against extremism—namely, the intentional pursuit of relationships built across deep difference. The inclusive quality of London Citizens is essential to the power that it holds.

The power of the London Citizens' Assembly (described in chapter 2) did not lie in the fact that it assembled six thousand citizens. After all, that number is exceeded every Friday at East London Mosque and every Sunday at Pentecostal mega-churches. Rather, the distinctive power of this gathering lay in the fact that it brought together citizens reflecting the diversity of the city's poorest neighborhoods. The power of the alliance is not held in one place but is dispersed among a range of institutions. Because the practice of community organizing requires the members of those institutions to take action and to assemble, the active assent of each of its various institutions and traditions is required for the ends the alliance pursues. This makes its "hijacking" virtually impossible.

What Bretherton calls "antipolitical populism" has the opposite qualities. It builds a movement in which power is not dispersed, institutions have no place, and little is demanded of citizens: "[Antipolitical populism] seeks to simplify rather than complexify the political space. It advocates direct forms of democracy in order to circumvent the need for deliberative processes and the representation of multiple interests in the formation of political judgments. The leader rules by direct consent without the hindrance of democratic checks and balances or the representation of different interests." Written in 2015, Bretherton's description foreshadows Trump's approach to governance: "The throwing off of established authority structures is the prelude to the giving over of authority to the one and the giving up of responsibility for the many. The goal of anti-political populism is personal withdrawal from public life so as to be free to pursue private self-interests rather than public mutual interests.[3]

As I will argue in chapter 6, it was the Tea Party's embrace of "anti-political populism," and its lack of interest in the vital role of mediating institutions that left it vulnerable to being overwhelmed by the "fake populism" of Donald Trump.

DOES ORGANIZING PROVIDE A PLATFORM FOR REGRESSIVE GROUPS?

Related to the fear of "hijacking" is a concern that community organizing provides a platform for institutions with regressive views. Sukhwant Dhaliwal, the former leader of Southall Black Sisters, has leveled this criticism against community organizing. In a lecture for the Open University she claimed that, for Citizens UK, "if you're an organization that can turn out large numbers of people to demonstrations and you can pay dues, then you're in." She argues that this has led to a situation in which "there are an array of religious organizations involved in that alliance. . . . East London mosque is the right-leaning Muslim organization in there, the Catholic Church is probably quite problematic as well."[4]

As David Barclay observes, the logic of Dhaliwal's argument is that "progressive tests" should be applied to any group that joins a community organizing alliance in order to keep out those with "problematic," "right-leaning," or extreme views. However, Barclay contends, this strategy is counterproductive. Declaring that whole groups in society are "beyond engagement" because of their (real, imagined, or potential) extremism reduces the chance that their views will be moderated:

> The problem with such an approach is that by precluding any possibility of building political friendships with those considered "beyond engagement," large sections of society (and in particular religious groups) are condemned to a position of isolation. Compounding this issue is the lack of evidence that "progressive tests" are in any way effective in transforming the undesirable behaviors or beliefs of those classed as unsuitable for partnership. Rather than incentivizing "better" behavior, it seems likely that such snubs only serve to

embolden exactly the more conservative or reactionary forces which are deemed to be problematic in the first place, leading to further segregation and retrenchment.[5]

Instead of "progressive tests," community organizing applies a "relational test" to prospective members by asking not what they believe but whether they are willing to respect and work with people who are different. All new members of London Citizens have to sign a "letter of understanding" upon joining. That letter contains a number of expected actions on the part of the member organizations, including the requirement that "each London Citizens member institution should be relational in all that they do and stand out as friendly and inclusive in their neighborhood. We are judged by what we do, not what we say. They should feel responsible for the wellbeing of their local community by reaching out to their neighbors in pursuit of the common good." Several of the community organizers whom Barclay interviewed described this ability to work with others in the alliance as a key test for possible new partners in their particular area. One man said, "I would only recruit organizations that I felt could be part of a broad-based organization [and] could share common values with other organizations." He added that "that willingness to find a shared agenda is also the thing that attracts people to it."[6]

Inevitably, London Citizens' willingness to engage with such a wide variety of institutions has generated tensions. But, as Barclay's research shows, they have largely been creative tensions. Precisely because the diverse groups in the alliance are in face-to-face relationship, engaged in action that builds trust and solidarity, there is an opportunity to address prejudice in a way that the standard practices of the progressive left cannot. Barclay's research offers a specific example:

In Citizens UK the key testing point has been in relation to the East London Mosque, whose membership has caused significant criticism, particularly from the Jewish community. When speaking about their experience of the Mosque, however, one interviewee explained that "they've always sat at the table with everybody else and been prepared to work with everybody else. . . . I'm sure it's changed the leadership who have engaged with it, absolutely." Another argued, "In terms of somewhere like the East London Mosque I've found the accusations

about what they're supposed to do not to be true. It makes you realise
... until we really know people how can we judge that?"[7]

As Barclay observes, it is not only left-wing activists who impose progressive tests. Increasingly on the right of politics, concerns about Islam
have led to a desire for such tests so that those whose views are deemed
"extremist" can be excluded.

On the right as on the left, the use of such progressive tests assumes
that intolerance and extremism are highly contagious, and therefore that
the best response is the political quarantining of those whose views are
deemed unacceptable. The work of London Citizens, by contrast, assumes
that solidarity and respect are more contagious. Accordingly, the best antidote to intolerance and extremism is for people to have opportunities to
build relationships and discern common interests with those they previously mistrusted.

Regrettably, the surge in far-right populism vindicates London Citizens' assumption. For it is when people are not in relationship across deep
difference, and when their institutions are either weak or self-segregating,
that there is the greatest danger of extremism being contagious. By contrast, when a diverse range of institutions are in strong relationships with
one another—relationships that engage all the membership, not simply
the official leaders—solidarity and respect grow. It is not that the substantive differences of religion or belief melt away. Rather, organizing across
those differences leads those involved to discover and act on their common interests. In the process, they come to a deeper recognition of their
common humanity.

In the United States in particular, the spread of racist and xenophobic views has been greatly assisted by "shock jocks" on the radio, the constant diet of misinformation on Fox News, and the self-segregating nature
of social media. The "no-platforming" policies of the progressive left have
been useless in abating this tide of prejudice. They have compounded the
original problem, namely, the lack of opportunity for people to come together across deep difference to build a common life.

In the wake of Trump's election victory, Columbia University profes-
sor Mark Lilla penned a blistering attack on the progressive left for their
refusal to set aside issues of dispute and build coalitions on shared concerns. He urges progressive colleagues to "impose no purity tests on those
you would convince" and accept that they will never agree with people on

everything. As Lilla writes, "That's to be expected in a democracy. One ef-fect of engaging in social movements tied to identity is that you've been surrounded by the like-minded and like-faced and like-educated."[8] He provides an example that is particularly salient in the US context. While abortion is the social issue about which Lilla cares the most (believing it should be "safe and legal virtually on every square inch of American soil"), he decries his fellow progressives for "driv[ing] pro-lifers out of the gar-den and into the waiting arms of the radical right."

One can hardly deny the polling evidence: Both white evangelical support for Trump and the unexpected hesitancy of African American and Latino voters to support Clinton are at least in part explained by the Democratic Party's decision to signal its disapproval of religious vot-ers who are more hostile to abortion. Lilla recounts a revealing moment at the Democratic Party's 1992 national convention: "That was the year Robert P. Casey, the Catholic Pennsylvania governor who had worked re-lentlessly to expand social services in his state and was very pro-union, asked to address the convention and present a pro-life plank to the plat-form, even though he knew it would be defeated. His request was denied. That sent a strong signal to working-class Catholic and evangelical vot-ers that if they did not fall into line on this one issue they were no longer welcome in the party."

By 2016, in fact, someone with Casey's opinions would struggle to se-cure endorsement as a candidate at the Democratic National Committee. As Lilla observes, the aftermath of Trump's victory has not been encour-aging to those who want to make the movement against him as inclu-sive and broad-based as possible. "In the run-up to the Women's March on Washington in January 2017 the same thing [as happened to Casey] happened to religious feminist groups that wanted to express their disgust with Donald Trump but were opposed to abortion," he writes. "They were disinvited. And one more bridge was burned."[9]

Within IAF and Citizens UK, abortion is treated as a "wedge issue." The institutions in membership have deeply held, divergent views on the question. Being part of a broad-based alliance does not require them to agree and is compatible with their campaigning vigorously (outside of the alliance's activities) for their diverse positions. A Roman Catholic parish in IAF does not have to choose between campaigning on the living wage and campaigning against abortion, any more than a Student Union has to choose between campaigning on the living wage and participating in a pro-choice demonstration. Both institutions simply agree that campaigns on the latter issue will not be waged under the IAF umbrella.

While working together on shared issues will not remove the deeply held disagreements on abortion, it may well improve the quality of the debate. It is possible to hold a position at either extreme of the abortion debate and yet to comprehend why thoughtful people take the opposing view. The unwillingness to engage your opponents removes an opportunity to convince a fellow citizen of the value of your point of view and to understand how your own side may be needlessly alienating others. It also removes the opportunity to act together on the other issues on which you *do* agree. As Lilla observes, such "self-sabotage" is an essential part of the story of Trump's victory.

IS "SELF-INTEREST" TOO CYNICAL?

A feature of community organizing that alienates many otherwise sympathetic people is its focus on self-interest. On the surface, Alinsky has a deeply cynical view of human motivation. As he wrote in *Reveille for Radicals*, "I've been asked, for example, why I never talk to a Catholic priest or a Protestant minister in terms of the Judaeo-Christian ethic or the Ten Commandments or the Sermon on the Mount. I never talk in those terms. Instead I approach them on the basis of their own self-interest, the welfare of their Church, even its physical property."[10]

Alinsky's desire to unmask the power dynamics hiding behind moral rhetoric left him unable or unwilling to articulate the positive ethical stance that so clearly drove both his work and the work of many of the grassroots leaders with whom he worked. In the fascinating correspondence between Alinsky and the French Catholic philosopher Jacques Maritain, the latter rightly refuses Alinsky's "contrarian self-descriptions" and urges him instead to recognize that "all [Maritain's] fighting effort as an organizer is quickened *in reality* by *love for the human being, and for God,* though you refuse to admit it, by a kind of inner *pudeur*."[11] As Maritain observed, it is impossible to rationalize Alinsky's own life choices in terms of the cynical view of human motivation he offered. Any account of "self-interest" that makes it synonymous with selfishness is refuted not only by the evident motivations of Alinsky and his fellow organizers but also by those who work (whether on a paid or voluntary basis) in the institutions that constitute an alliance such as London Citizens.

In his 1993 study of community organizing in the United States, Jay MacLeod suggested that self-interest had been superseded in the lexicon of organizing, "yielding" to a more values-based discourse. (He dates the change to the mid-1970s, when Ed Chambers succeeded Saul Alinsky as Director of IAF.) "The key word in church or broad-based organizing is values. People are still organized around issues based on self-interest, but church-based organizations are also built upon the values, visions, beliefs and commitments which stem from religious traditions. Even old-school organizers are coming to appreciate that churches work better from their own values and vision than from self-interest. Self-interest has yielded to the values of justice, concern for the poor, the dignity of the person, participation and respect for diversity as a motivation for involvement."[12]

Anyone attending IAF training in 1993, or the training of its many affiliates in 2015, will find that IAF's conception of "self-interest" remains central to the approach and is made explicit in its teaching of religious and civic leaders. However, under the leadership of Ed Chambers and, more recently, of Ernesto Cortés and Michael Gecan, community organizing has developed a more nuanced and accurate understanding of the nature of human motivation.

As I argued in chapter 3, we cannot give an adequate account of the "interests" of human beings without reference to the "goods" they have reason to value. An excessively cynical account of self-interest is both empirically and conceptually problematic—for both the value-based institutions at the heart of organizing alliances and the individuals who participate in them.

In *Cold Anger*, Mary Beth Rogers describes the transition within IAF's organizing away from Alinsky's excessively cynical account of human motivation—and toward an understanding of self-interest that made room for the values and vocations of institutions of their members. As she explains, this transition led IAF to incorporate ethical and theological reflection into its training process. In the words of Cortés, organizing became about "values and vision" as well as "action and issues." It developed a balanced understanding of self-interest that avoided both Alinsky's excessive cynicism and the equal and opposite tendency of religious and moral idealists to underestimate the complexity and diversity of human motivations.[13] This point is illustrated by an early TELCO campaign that concerned the quality of cleaning, catering, and care at Newham General Hospital. The low quality of cleaning was a constant theme of my "one-to-ones" in the Anglican Parish of the Divine Compassion, Plaistow and Canning Town, the first parish in which I organized. As we formed an action team with members of St. Margaret's Catholic Parish, Canning Town, we built a relationship with the hospital cleaners' trade union branch. We soon learned that the cleaners had gone through a classic "outsourcing" process. Initially they had worked for the National Health Service (NHS). They had then lost their NHS jobs, and many had been re-employed, at much lower rates of pay, by cleaning contractors. The outsourcing process had assumed that human motivation was fundamentally selfish—and failed to recognize that the cleaners had previously offered a level of goodwill that could not be extracted by ever more penal forms of oversight. When the cleaners had been paid and treated as members of the NHS, they had understood themselves as co-workers with a shared vocation of patient care. When the NHS behaved in a way that made clear it did not share that understanding, the quality of their work declined dramatically.

In Newham General Hospital, the assumption that cleaners had only selfish motivations led to a process of outsourcing that removed their sense of vocation. By contrast, when the accounting firm KPMG started to pay a living wage to all its low-wage employees, it discovered that productivity increased.[14] The impact on productivity and retention rates generated savings in excess of the higher salary costs of the living wage.

While Alinsky (in his more provocative moments) conflates self-interest and selfishness, the interests that actually motivate those involved in community organizing mix concern for their own wellbeing and that of their families with their moral and spiritual values, and indeed the moral and spiritual visions of the institutions of which they are a part.

Chris Shanahan has argued that even a nuanced version of self-interest is an inadequate ethical foundation for community organizing. In *A Theology of Community Organising* he urges community organizers to abandon the term "self-interest" altogether and to develop a more robust and unified moral and spiritual narrative:

> In spite of its enduring hold on community organizers on both sides of the Atlantic, I suggest that even a carefully rephrased commitment to self-interest cannot provide an adequate foundation on which to build a liberative theology of community organizing. . . .

It would not be socially credible or ethically acceptable to tie an interfaith community organization in a superdiverse society to a particular doctrinal template or a specific faith tradition. However . . . I do want to suggest that it is possible to provide a theology of community organizing and faith-based community organisers with a unifying and socially progressive ethical foundation on which to build an inclusive people's organization.[15]

It is no coincidence that Shanahan's two recommendations (removing self-interest as a foundation for common action and urging an interfaith theology of community organizing) appear side by side. For they both flow from the same mistake: namely, an unwillingness to live with the *negotiated* pluralism at the heart of community organizing.

In practice, Shanahan's proposals, like those of many political liberals, would eliminate the diversity he celebrates. If community organizing were founded on an "interfaith theology" of the kind Shanahan seeks to develop, it would alienate the very groups that it has a unique capacity to unite—that is, those groups whose differences in worldview are deepest but who are nonetheless able to build relationships and trust because those different worldviews motivate a set of shared activities.

To stop engaging with the self-interest of different organizations and communities and to seek instead to form a unified moral narrative (like Shanahan's "interfaith theology"), is to cease to engage with the depth of genuine difference between parties being brought together. Part of the power of community organizing comes from its appreciation that these differences are indeed deep and that it takes time to draw people together and to draw a common interest out of their diverse interests and perspectives. The consistent experience of congregations in the alliance is that going deeper into the distinctive beliefs and cultures of different religions and denominations is the key to engaging an increasing breadth of participation from each community. This is why congregations involved in community organizing are so resistant to the call made by Shanahan for an abandonment of the language of self-interest and any dilution of their commitment to their (often mutually incompatible) theological commitments.

Like the political liberalism of John Rawls, the "open-ended" theology advocated by Shanahan is deceptive in its inclusivity. For it includes only those willing to dilute, or even deny altogether, the distinctive truth claims of their own theological positions. The rhetoric of Shanahan's text is relentlessly negative about any exclusive claims to truth. Shanahan's selective appeal to the Christian tradition (playing up texts about social justice and playing down any exclusive claims to truth) is, we are told, "shaped by an *a priori* commitment to liberative action." Not surprisingly, if people decide in advance to interpret the Christian faith in a way that they deem "liberative," they will end up with the results they want and can dismiss recalcitrant aspects of Scripture and Tradition as "theological exclusivism."[16]

Shanahan is in fact imposing his own theological commitments, which hold exclusive religious truth claims in low esteem, on an alliance in which the congregations with the greatest number of racially and economically excluded members are in fact much more theologically conservative. In the name of "radical inclusion," those who reject such theological liberalism turn out to be unwelcome. Shanahan's "interfaith theology of organizing" condemns as "exclusive" the mosques, Roman Catholic parishes, and Pentecostal and Baptist churches at the heart of the UK and US alliances. The real achievement of community organizing is its ability to draw together a greater variety of religions and beliefs, precisely because it engages with the self-interest of each on its own terms and provides a space hospitable to a much deeper pluralism. Yet such a pluralism constantly needs to be renegotiated. The attempt to formulate an "interfaith theology of organizing" in fact imposes homogeneity on the diversity of interests and worldviews that the practice brings together. In the long run, as we have seen in the case of left-liberal movements like Occupy, this will create a movement dominated by middle-class activists (who wish to work on behalf of those in need) rather than a genuinely populist alliance.

The focus on self-interest—when we appreciate that it refers to the actual (altruistic as well as selfish) interests of each person and institution rather than the excessively cynical account given by late capitalist economics—is essential to maintaining the negotiated pluralism at the heart of community organizing. Attempts to blend those diverse interests and commitments into a single moral narrative make it harder to sustain a truly inclusive movement.

I turn now from a discussion of the desirability of organizing to an exploration of its effectiveness. In the wake of the Obama presidency, the most obvious challenge is the following: Has not organizing already been tried—and shown to fail—at a national level?

HASN'T ORGANIZING ALREADY BEEN TRIED?

For veterans of community organizing, the rise of Barack Obama provided an unusual sensation. The work of IAF and Citizens UK had previously been an undertheorized, underreported phenomenon, precisely because it was undertaken far from the "Washington beltway" or the "Westminster bubble." Suddenly this work came into fashion. "Community organizing" was on the lips of nearly every commentator and policy-maker. Obama's speeches and writings extolled the potential of community organizing and its capacity for engaging citizens who felt alienated from electoral politics and for bringing unity where there was previously growing polarization. As President, Obama promised, he would harness this potential to change America for the better. Announcing his candidacy in 2007, he declared:

> After all, every four years, candidates from both parties make similar promises, and I expect this year will be no different. . . . But too many times, after the election is over, and the confetti is swept away, all those promises fade from memory, and the lobbyists and the special interests move in, and people turn away, disappointed as before, left to struggle on their own.
>
> That is why this campaign can't only be about me. It must be about us—it must be about what we can do together. This campaign must be the occasion, the vehicle, of your hopes, and your dreams. It will take your time, your energy, and your advice—to push us forward when we're doing right, and to let us know when we're not. This campaign has to be about reclaiming the meaning of citizenship, restoring our sense of common purpose, and realizing that few obstacles can withstand the power of millions of voices calling for change.[17]

Why does the United States feel even further from these noble aspirations in 2017 than it did a decade earlier?

Ta-Nehisi Coates argues that Obama's failure flowed from his inability to address the racism at the heart of American society. This same failure to name and confront the structural injustices in American society—a "raceless antiracism"—"marks the modern left, from the New Democrat Bill Clinton to the socialist Bernie Sanders." Few national liberal politicians, Coates claims, "have shown any recognition that there is something systemic and particular in the relationship between black people and their country that might require specific policy solutions."

As Coates observes, Trump's racism was evident before he declared his candidacy. Indeed, he rose to political prominence through the role he played in the "birther" movement, which denied that Obama was a legitimate president. While such racism continued in Trump's campaign, it has reached new heights in his presidency.[18] Coates claims that the mainstream response to Trump's election continues in this tradition of "raceless antiracism" by failing to name and confront the real reasons for his rise. "Asserting that Trump's rise was primarily powered by cultural resentment and economic reversal has become *de rigueur* among white pundits and thought leaders," he writes. This follows a long tradition in American politics of treating poverty among whites with a seriousness absent when it is faced by blacks: "Black workers suffer because it was and is our lot. But when white workers suffer, something in nature has gone awry. And so an opioid epidemic among mostly white people is greeted with calls for compassion and treatment, as all epidemics should be, while a crack epidemic among mostly black people is greeted with scorn and mandatory minimums. Sympathetic op-ed columns and articles are devoted to the plight of working-class whites when their life expectancy plummets to levels that, for blacks, society has simply accepted as normal."[19] Explaining the surge in Trump support in terms of structural racism and the alienation of the white working class need not be mutually exclusive. Coates is clearly right in identifying racism as a central dynamic in the rise of right-wing populism. However, the narrowness of Trump's victory means that a number of different counterfactuals are true: It is true that if more white working-class voters in Michigan and Wisconsin had voted for Clinton *or* if the predicted "Latino surge" for Clinton had materialized *or* if African Americans had turned out for Clinton in 2016 in the same numbers they did for Obama in 2008, Donald Trump would not have been elected.[20] An adequate account of Trump's victory must begin with an account of the country's deep-seated racial inequalities. But it will also need to explain the alienation and anger felt by many working-class whites *and* the demotivation of so many African American and Latino voters in the face of an overtly racist candidate.

During the election campaign, as is well known, Hilary Clinton described those supporting Donald Trump as a "basket of deplorables," a

phrase that was soon emblazoned with pride on baseball caps at his supporters' rallies. Rather tellingly, Clinton uttered this phrase at a donors'
dinner. The attitude and the setting echoed gaffes by Mitt Romney and
Barack Obama in previous presidential election campaigns. This made it
all the easier for Trump to sustain the narrative that "Washington elites"
from both parties despised working-class white voters while remaining in
hock to wealthy donors who had both caused the financial crash and appeared to have shared so little in the suffering it caused.

Moreover, a closer examination of the demographics of Trump's victory shows a third significant factor. This was the failure of the Clinton
campaign to energize African American and Latino voters, even in the
face of an overtly racist campaign by her main opponent.

One reason all three groups of voters were not motivated to support the Democrats was the (perhaps inevitable) failure of the Obama
administration to live up to its community organizing rhetoric. Back in
2010, Jeffrey Stout had expressed concern that a campaign that used the
rhetoric of community organizing and social transformation would raise
dangerous expectations. Reflecting subsequently on the Obama presidency, he noted that Obama's claim was "that the crisis of democracy
is a matter of an imbalance of power between ordinary citizens and the
ruling elites. The claim struck a chord because it is true."[21] However,
Stout was pessimistic about Obama's capacity for delivering the change
he had promised. Despite the language of community organizing, Stout
argued, the administration was still beholden to the "ruling elites." As
evidence he cited Obama's "top-down" response to the financial crisis
and to health care reform. In assembling his team of economic advisors,
Obama chose establishment figures such as Robert Rubin and Lawrence
Summers over Nobel laureate Joseph Stiglitz, who favored "including
ordinary citizens in deliberations on major issues concerning economic
policy."[22] Likewise, on the issue of health care reform, Organizing for
America (Obama's community organizing movement) was in fact engaged in mobilizing support for positions thrashed out by politicians and
vested interest groups behind closed doors rather than engaging citizens
in a genuine deliberative process.

This criticism may seem unfair. Is it realistic to imagine a truly deliberative "bottom-up" process being initiated by a president required to
focus on assembling a majority within a hostile Congress, one who had to

act swiftly to prevent a global financial crisis from descending into full-scale economic meltdown? Does not Stout's critique underestimate the achievement of the Obama administration in deriving health care reform through the credit crunch and ameliorating the worst effects of it?

All presidents have limited room for political maneuvering, and the first African American President had to contend with a constant drumbeat of (implicitly or explicitly) racist abuse portraying him as a closet Muslim and denying his legitimacy as a candidate. However, Stout's argument does help us to address the claim that, in Obama's presidency, community organizing was tried and found to fail. Whether or not Obama could realistically have done anything else, it is clear that his presidency did not exemplify the kind of authentic populism for which I am arguing.

It is revealing that Obama described his experience of organizing as one in which he learned "things that would help me bring about real change," as if "real change" was something that would be delivered somewhere else.[23] According to Obama's own rhetoric, the real change that is needed can be delivered only from the grassroots. "When classmates in college asked me just what it was that a community organizer did, I couldn't answer them directly," he writes. "Instead, I'd pronounce on the need for change. . . . Change wouldn't come from the top, I would say. Change will come from a mobilized grass roots."[24]

Obama was caught in a contradiction. According to his own rhetoric, the White House was not the place from which this kind of transformation could or should begin. Stout captures the paradox well: "Alinsky taught that democracy is alive in the habits of the people only when they organize themselves effectively and hold corporate bosses and government officials responsible for the arrangements and policies that are in place. Electing a president who believes that Alinsky was right is hardly the same thing as building an effective culture of accountability by something like Alinsky's means."[25] None of this is to decry the vocation of elected politicians in general or the accomplishments of Obama in particular. While the renewal of civil society cannot be initiated by politicians, politicians can actively support such a renewal. Obama's rhetoric promised a kind of renewal that he could not deliver. There remains a question as to how elected politicians might support such renewal. I want to explore that question through an evaluation of the "Big Society" vision of David Cameron, who was Britain's prime minister for most of the Obama presidency.

ORGANIZING AND THE "BIG SOCIETY"

Community organizing reached national prominence in the United Kingdom in the 2010 General Election campaign. Conservative Party leader David Cameron campaigned on the theme of a "Big Society." In terms that echoed an analysis of organizing, he argued for a strengthened civil society, which he said should be seen as "The First Sector not the Third Sector" alongside the state and the market.

The dynamics of the 2010 campaign were unusual. The weakened position of sitting Prime Minister Gordon Brown led him to agree to three televised debates—and to a "fourth debate" in which he appeared alongside Cameron and Liberal Democrat leader Nick Clegg at a national Citizens UK assembly. (In the 2015 and 2017 elections, the sitting premier refused to attend any of these.) At the Citizens UK assembly, Cameron told the gathering, "You are the 'Big Society'" and promised to fund five thousand community organizers to challenge poverty.

The implementation of the Big Society program, and attempts by the Labour Party to develop its own community organizing movement, ran into similar challenges to those encountered by the Obama administration and its Organizing for America movement. The renewal of civil society cannot be a "top-down" program; a movement tied to a particular political party cannot become a broad-based alliance like IAF or Citizens UK.

Upon his election, Cameron chose not to award the community organizing contract to Citizens UK. As Madeline Bunting observed, this was hardly surprising: "This was always the toughest test of the big society policy: what politician—let alone government—ever gives power away? What civil service, trained to manage risk, is ever prepared to lose control? Again and again these questions have cropped up, and the big society advocates in government have insisted that they are serious about relinquishing power, however messy and unmanageable the consequences. Or . . . maybe not."[26] In the event, this was probably the best outcome for Citizens UK. There had been some concern within the organization about bidding for this government contract, as it broke the alliance's rule of remaining financially independent. However, a combination of the scale of the opportunity and a reluctance to appear truculent in the face of such a generous offer led Citizens UK to submit a bid. Perhaps the most compelling argument for bidding was the danger that a large-scale rival to

Citizens UK would become established and use watered-down community organizing methods.

Whether or not Citizens UK was right to submit a bid, the outcome was in fact the best possible one for the movement. It was not co-opted by winning the contract, an outcome that would have severely diminished its independence and credibility (particularly given the impact of subsequent government spending cuts on the neighborhoods where it is rooted). But the bid that was finally accepted (that of a consortium led by the charity Locality) had shrunk to a scale that would barely have an impact on Citizens' work. Six years on, the expansion of Citizens UK has been done at a slower pace and in all new cities is now fully funded by "hard money." As we shall see, this method of winning resources provides a much more solid basis for authentic organizing.

The story of the community organizing contract indicates the difficulty facing politicians who seek to harness the potential of the movement. The dynamics Bunting identified, of promises to devolve power being made by a candidate in a campaign and subverted when in office, will be familiar to observers of the devolution of power by Tony Blair's government to a Scottish Parliament, a Welsh Senedd, and an elected mayor and Assembly in Greater London. In each case, the impulse to devolve power was subverted by an attempt to impose unwelcome candidates (for Scottish and Welsh first minister and for mayor of London). In each case, Blair was unsuccessful because there had been a legally binding devolution of power—and so, for example, his attempt to prevent Ken Livingstone from becoming mayor simply led Livingstone to run successfully as an independent against the Blair-endorsed Labour candidate.

In the case of community organizing, it is far less obvious how a government could devolve power in a way that neither compromised the independence of the organizing alliance nor would be subverted by the pressures and temptations of elective politics. The central challenge posed to politicians by organizing is to cease to imagine themselves as the initiators of all the necessary changes. As those involved in community organizing will attest, how the institutions of government *respond* to independently organized citizens (especially when they are organized around religion and belief) is as important as what these institutions seek to initiate. David Cameron's Big Society agenda had the laudable aim of strengthening civil society, as distinct from both state and market. But it seemed to operate according to a binary model: government either initiated Big Society projects, which required a response from civil society, or it withdrew public services and expected civil society to make up the gap. A more respectful engagement between the state and civil society would require government to think about how to respond creatively when civil society took the initiative.

The record of the Cameron government bears out this point. If we take him at his word, Cameron believed that Citizens UK was a practical embodiment of the Big Society. His instinctive response, however, was an initiative. The £15 million spent on state-sponsored community organizers has done nothing to help the movement develop; indeed, it is likely that if Citizens UK had received the money, it could have done lasting damage to its integrity and credibility. By contrast, the decision of Mayor Boris Johnson to follow his Labour predecessors in attending London Citizens' accountability assemblies and supporting its Living Wage Campaign was hugely helpful to the movement. Knowing that Conservative incumbents were willing to do business with London Citizens increased the alliance's negotiating power with Labour politicians and the credibility of the alliance when it demanded that employers pay a Living Wage. Indeed, it was Johnson's decision to follow his Labour predecessors in attending such assemblies that established the assemblies securely as a regular feature of London mayoral elections.

By the same token, the decision of Brown, Cameron, and Clegg to attend Citizens UK's 2010 General Election Accountability Assembly helped the alliance to grow into a genuinely nationwide movement, increasingly funded by "hard money." Being willing to be held to account publicly has helped Citizens UK much more than £15 million of state funding. This is a powerful illustration of my larger point: A creative, respectful response to civil society when *it* takes the initiative is far more helpful than any number of government programs to promote "community engagement."

In contrast, Cameron's betrayal of his public promise to attend another such assembly before the 2015 election significantly reduced the likelihood of these assemblies' becoming regular features of UK General elections (in the way that they are now an established feature of London's mayoral elections). Ironically, like the failure of Obama's attempt to renew civil society in the United States, the failure of Cameron's Big Society initiative can be attributed to its excessive statism and its inability to live out a vision of government as something genuinely responsive to a robust and independent civil society.

While there are limits to the ways in which the state can support the development of bottom-up movements such as IAF and Citizens UK, other allies can certainly help community organizing to flourish. Larger-scale civil society institutions (such as regional trade unions and Catholic, Anglican, Episcopalian, and Lutheran dioceses and synods) can invest in their local community organizing alliances, providing a source of hard money that complements the membership dues of more local units. Such additional funding should be tied not to campaign outputs (lest they distort the movement every bit as much as "soft money") but to targets for institutional development. If such investment takes the form of match-funding local membership dues, it can also increase the amount of locally raised hard money. In order to engage more fully with community organizing, trade unions will need to recover some of the movement's earlier traditions by replacing bureaucratic decision-making processes with more relational ones and being willing to form broad-based alliances with non-secular groups.

On both sides of the Atlantic, national governments have been neither able nor willing to generate a genuinely inclusive populism. By contrast, the institutions of civil society could do more to invest in community organizing, a practice that could do much to make those institutions more resilient.

The two remaining criticisms of organizing relate to the effectiveness of the day-to-day work of IAF and Citizens UK and the extent to which it lives up to its rhetorical promise.

DOES ORGANIZING PRACTICE WHAT IT PREACHES?

The theory of community organizing states that power lies with the institutions that constitute its broad-based alliances. In practice, many of those interviewed said that a great deal of the power lay with the paid community organizers. These organizers face a constant temptation to develop and initiate action at a pace that goes beyond the self-interest and experience of grassroots leaders.

The risk is not that the paid organizers will somehow "hijack" the movement, directing it to unsavory ends. As I argued earlier, the structure of the local alliances in Citizens UK and IAF means that there is no serious danger of action being taken that conflicts with the values that those institutions share. Rather, the danger is that organizers might initiate actions on issues that (although they accord with the values of its constituent institutions) have not emerged from conversations expressing the interests and decisions of their members.

The temptation for organizers to take short cuts is considerable. In the face of worsening material conditions for many of the poorest citizens and the rise in far-right populism, there is an understandable impatience on the part of organizers to expand the alliances more quickly—and thus to win more substantial victories on issues such as the living wage, affordable housing, and better treatment of migrants and refugees.

Drawing on his extensive experience of popular movements in Latin American, Pope Francis cautions against such impatience. In a section of *Evangelii Gaudium* titled "Time Is Greater Than Space," he warns:

> One of the faults which we occasionally observe in sociopolitical activity is that spaces and power are preferred to time and processes. Giving priority to space means madly attempting to keep everything together in the present, trying to possess all the spaces of power and of self-assertion; it is to crystallize processes and presume to hold them back. Giving priority to time means being concerned about initiating processes rather than possessing spaces....
>
> What we need ... is to give priority to actions which generate new processes in society and engage other persons and groups who can develop them to the point where they bear fruit in significant historical events—without anxiety, but with clear convictions and tenacity.[27]

When leaders of any institution give in to the temptation to move forward at a pace that is unsustainable, and when they fail to share their power (implementing a top-down agenda rather than allowing it to be shaped by the interests of their members), the long-term effect is to weaken that institution. Unless the pace of leadership development is sustainable and the agenda is genuinely shaped by the membership, those members will not take responsibility for the organization, and the people running it will in the end burn out. This is as true for community organizing alliances as it is for its individual congregations or trade unions.

As Jeffrey Stout observes, organizers are keenly aware of the challenge:

> On the many occasions when I have discussed this matter with [Ernie] Cortés, . . . he has always underlined the importance of patience. In broad-based organizing that aspires ultimately to have a significant impact at the national and international levels, the standing temptation is, as he puts it, "to skip steps, to take short cuts." If the right sort of micro-organizational work is not being done, the macro-organizational work of connecting citizens' groups with one another in progressively wider networks will create only an illusion of democratic power. . . . If Cortés is right, it seems that high degrees of participation, vigilance, self-constraint, and patience on the part of organizers, leaders, and citizens will be required to scale up the organizational effort without sacrificing either effectiveness or internal accountability.[28]

Our research in London confirms Cortés's analysis and suggests that the necessary vigilance is indeed being practiced. While there is evidence of "short cuts" being taken, there is also evidence that they are being corrected. There is a self-correcting dynamic within the organizing process. Precisely because short cuts are ultimately self-defeating, in the longer term it is patient organizing that builds the more powerful alliances. In the places where community organizing has stayed close to the interests of the poorest residents, more leaders are developed and more secure funding becomes available.

An example of this is the changing way in which the organization in the UK is financed. At the time of this writing, the East London chapter of the alliance has managed to increase the proportion of organizer time funded by hard money to around 50 percent, and new chapters in other cities are often securing 100 percent of their funding from hard money—a dramatic shift in the alliance's practice. The patient organizing by Fr. Sean Connolly in the Catholic Parish of Manor Park is a case in point. In August 2017 the parish decided to invest in its own part-time community organizer to harness the potential of organizing to strengthen the institution and to act on issues of local concern. The hard money for this has come directly from the giving of worshipers in one of London's most deprived and diverse neighborhoods. The giving, in turn, is a powerful illustration of the potential of patient organizing, rooted in the interests of the poorest, to build a genuinely populist movement.

Across Citizens UK there is an increasing focus on the potential of the practice of organizing to strengthen institutions. This began in London Citizens' churches through the Congregational Development Learning Community run in partnership with the Centre for Theology and Community (CTC) and based on the "hallmarks of an organized church" listed in Chapter 2. More recently, Citizens UK and CTC have begun working in partnership with the Movement for Reform Judaism (MRJ) to apply these insights to synagogues. The impact of these two projects is generating an appetite for similar work in mosques, schools, and other chapters of Citizens UK.

The self-correcting dynamic we see in London Citizens is evident in the organizing movement more generally. Michael Gecan and Ernie Cortés, the veteran organizers who co-direct IAF, emphasize that "all organizing is disorganizing and re-organizing." According to Cortés, a good "rule of thumb" is that some process of disorganizing and reorganizing will need to occur every two or three years. This recurrent process ensures that, as well as taking action, organizers are continually focused on deepening the roots of the work in each institution, with growing teams of local leaders involved.[29]

DOES ORGANIZING EMBODY A GENUINE PLURALISM?

As I pointed out in chapter 2, our research also found concerns among some participants in organizing that it instrumentalizes the religions and beliefs of those who constitute the alliance. This raises the question of whether community organizing succeeds in embodying a genuine pluralism. Are the distinctive convictions of its member institutions honored, or does organizing simply co-opt these organizations to an alien political agenda? The concern came up in a number of Barclay's interviews, particularly with religious participants:

> One Christian interviewee explained that the culture of some Citizens UK meetings "can feel a little bit tokenistic sometimes by just throwing in a little Bible reading, a Qur'anic reading in the beginning," and that he has "cringed in the past when we had a multifaith choir." For him opportunities for people to express their own religious identities or motivations, whether through their institutional identification, their

dress, or their testimony, were entirely to be welcomed. But situations in which people were claiming to speak for a particular religious tradition or project a certain set of values and beliefs onto the group were more likely to create problems.... [He continued,] "I think that the language and the articulation of these things is quite tricky without becoming tokenistic or equally cringeworthy."[30]

Some nonreligious critics of organizing have raised the opposite concern, namely, that it is a "front" by which religious groups can impose their worldviews on the wider society. (One senior atheist politician was convinced that London Citizens was an "evangelical Christian plot.")

NEGOTIATING PLURALISM: THE CAMPAIGN FOR A CREDIT CAP

Such concerns are perhaps inevitable. Because secularizing liberalism conceives of itself as a neutral mediator between irreconcilable visions of the good life, its proponents cannot imagine how a practice can be genuinely rooted in those diverse visions and yet form substantive policy positions on issues such as the living wage, affordable housing, and hospitality to migrants and refugees.

As I argued in chapter 1, it is a mistake to conceive of the different religions and traditions in organizing as *simply* conflicting with one another, with liberalism functioning as some kind of umpire. Precisely because it has ruled out any substantive conceptions of the good life, secularizing liberalism has weakened the capacity of mediating institutions to resist the overweening power of market and state. What the traditions of mosque, synagogue, church, and trade union have in common is a resistance to the way both state and market can disempower and instrumentalize citizens— with an overweening state reducing them to clients of an impersonal bureaucracy and an overweening market reducing them to commodities in their work and consumers in their leisure time ("commodification").[31]

Without in any way diminishing the differences between the religious and ethical traditions of London Citizens' churches, mosques, synagogues, and trade unions, one can discern a common antipathy to commodification—an antipathy based on the assertion of the dignity of the human person and the importance of human and nonhuman ecology.

When London Citizens launched its anti-usury campaign (in the wake of the 2008 financial crisis), the *Guardian* observed: "It is telling that the lead voices in this new effort are from mosques, inner-city churches and synagogues. The politicians have been left looking flummoxed by the financial crisis, apparently desperate for normal business to resume as soon as possible. It has been left to [Pope Benedict XVI] to offer the most comprehensive critique of our devastated economic landscape, in his latest encyclical."[32] In that encyclical, *Caritas in Veritate*, the pope attacked the way financial systems had been cut loose from any vision of the common good: "The conviction that the economy must be autonomous, that it must be shielded from "influences" of a moral character, has led man to abuse the economic process in a thoroughly destructive way. In the long term, these convictions have led to economic, social and political systems that trample upon personal and social freedom, and are therefore unable to deliver the justice that they promise."[33]

As in the case of Pope Francis's *Laudato Sí*, Benedict's encyclical generated a response from other religions and beliefs, which demonstrates the possibility that common ground can be established without any denial of the distinctive convictions of each party. In a response to *Caritas in Veritate*, the senior Italian imam, Yayha Pallavancini, welcomed the way the encyclical recalled Christians to their own Scriptural teachings while recognizing the deep resonances with his own tradition: "Islamic ethics, from its origins, develops the common principles of the Abrahamic civilization as a whole aimed at providing 'joint satisfaction in material and spiritual needs.' For example, the Islamic ban on loans with interest (ribâ) also existed in ancient Christianity. As early as the 4th and 5th centuries, the Fathers of the Church, both Greeks and Latins, ardently opposed it based on both the Old Testament and the Gospel. . . . The West has wished to forget the economic principles present in religions, basically considering them to be, in modern times, a heritage of archaic thought."[34] As Pallavancini's comments indicate, there remains a difference between contemporary Church teaching on usury and Islamic ethics.

The differences as well as the resonances between the two traditions were reflected in the engagement between Christians and Muslims in London Citizens' successful campaign against exploitative payday lenders. On 2 January 2015, around thirty members of London Citizens processed from a North London church to the offices of Wonga, Britain's largest payday lender. The group included the Right Reverend Adrian Newman (the Church of England Bishop of Stepney) and Dr. Muhammad Abdul Bari, MBE (a key British Muslim leader and former secretary general of the Muslim Council of Britain), as well as members of Roman Catholic, Salvation Army, Methodist, and Quaker congregations and of the East London and Dar'ul Ummah Mosques. The group (which also included Jewish and nonreligious leaders) was gathered to celebrate the new cap on the cost of payday loans, which had come into force that day. Bishop Newman and Dr. Bari delivered a letter addressed to Andy Haste, the chair of the directors of Wonga, asking for a meeting to ensure that the company adhered to the spirit as well as the letter of the cap.

As Christian leaders involved in the campaign acknowledged, they had grown used to spiritualizing the Biblical language of "redemption"—forgetting that this metaphor is rooted in the remission of debt—and to ignoring the repeated attacks on exploitative lending in both the Bible and the teachings of the early Church. From around 2009, as the listening process in their churches revealed that increasing numbers of worshipers were falling prey to predatory lenders, Christians in London Citizens had to revisit these texts.[35] The fidelity of local Muslims to Qu'ranic teaching on usury both inspired and challenged Christian leaders in this process. While Christians relate to the Bible very differently from the way Muslims relate to the Qu'ran, the faithfulness of their Islamic neighbors encouraged Christians to attend more closely to Biblical injunctions on the way money is lent and borrowed.

In previous years, London Citizens had been involved in campaigns to ensure that financial products were accessible to faithful Muslims. Initially, many churches had supported the campaign solely as a means of ensuring that their Muslim neighbors had the necessary range of financial services. But, with the experience of predatory lenders such as Wonga and the aggressive marketing of credit by mainstream banks, Christians began to reflect on whether their own practice was sufficiently faithful. To help Christians reflect on the campaign, Luke Bretherton published "Neither a Borrower nor a Lender be," an essay that emphasized the central role of debt and remission in the Christian story. As Bretherton explained:

"At heart of the story of salvation we find the power of money and liberation from debt is a central concern. The admonition that we cannot serve both God and Mammon (Matt. 6:19–24) is not a trivial matter: the central drama of salvation history is an act of liberation from debt slavery. To put the pursuit of money before the welfare of people, and use money to re-enslave and exploit people, especially the poor and vulnerable, is to turn your back on God's salvation and deny in practice the revelation given in Scripture of who God is. Whereas to use money to serve the common good, and in particular to relieve the poor, is a mark of salvation."[36]

In this essay Bretherton traced the emergence in the pre-Reformation Church of a distinction (alien to Islam) between the lending of money at modest rates of interest (which the Church deemed licit if it was mutually beneficial) and "usury" (whereby one party profited by exploiting the other): "Trading agreements and loan contracts where both parties were expected to gain were one thing; lending at usury, where only the usurer could profit, was quite another. Even where a charge was deemed licit, the ideal for many Scholastic theologians was that such a charge be measured or moderate. For example, the Fourth Lateran Council (1215) condemned those who were 'heavy and excessive' in what they charged."[37]

While Christians in East London were inspired and challenged by their Muslim neighbors, the positions of adherents to each faith remained quite different. For most Muslims involved in Citizens UK (and indeed IAF), all lending at interest is understood as *haram* (forbidden) by faithful Muslims. As Vincent Rougeau explains, there are three reasons for this: (1) Interest or usury reinforces the tendency for wealth to accumulate in the hands of the few and thereby diminishes man's concern for his fellow man; (2) Islam does not allow gain from financial activity unless the beneficiary is also subject to the risk of potential loss; the legal guarantee of at least nominal interest would be viewed as guaranteed gain, and (3) Islam regards the accumulation of wealth through interest as selfish compared with accumulation through hard work and personal activity.[38]

As Bretherton's essay shows, these considerations have been echoed in Christian discussions of usury from the early Church onward, but since the medieval period it has usually been only excessive rates of interest that the Church has deemed unacceptable.

Because of these contrasting theological perspectives, there needed to be negotiation as well as mutual witness within the organizing process. The resulting policy platform allowed each community to retain the integrity of its own position while acting in ways that benefit those with related but distinct concerns.

Christians, and indeed people of other faiths and none, continued to support their Muslim neighbors in campaigning for accessible *shari'a*-compliant financial products. And mosques joined their non-Muslim neighbors in a successful campaign for the first legal cap on interest rates in the United Kingdom in over a century—although the financial products, even after this regulation, remained *haram* to faithful Muslims. Muslims involved in London Citizens recognized that, while these were not products they would ever wish to endorse, their regulation prevented something that Muslims and non-Muslims alike could recognize as a greater evil.[39]

ORGANIZING AND SPIRITUALITY

While such ethical convictions play an important part in the life of a community of faith, there is more to a church, mosque, or synagogue than can be captured by reviewing its beliefs. Religions do not exist merely to share a set of intellectual convictions. They are established to be places of *encounter* with God, in which the life of prayer and worship plays a central role.

There is, then, a particular concern that such communities will face when contemplating engagement with the organizing process—a concern that does not have any obvious correlate in secular institutions. The worry is that the distinctive mission of religious congregations, as places of spiritual encounter, will be diluted by such activism.

Australian church leader Sarah Bachelard argues that many churches' action for social justice has become "functionally atheistic," even in cases in which such action reflects the distinctive theological convictions of the church. Theological orthodoxy is not enough; the process by which a community discerns how to act must involve a living encounter with God. Bachelard writes that "in the context of the church's commitment to justice, the recovery of authentic practices of discernment is not just a matter of *preference*; it is not just that some of us prefer this way of decision-making rather than another. . . . It is a direct reflection of whether the church really does see itself as responsive to another Other—receiving itself and its vocation from God; or whether it is, for all its professions of faith, functionally *atheistic*."[40] This is why "integrating theology, spirituality, and action" is the first of the hallmarks of an organized church.

The experience of decades of organizing on each side of the Atlantic is unequivocal: unless action flows from the heart of the worshiping life of a church, mosque, or synagogue, it never moves beyond a small clique of enthusiasts. The majority of the members of a religious congregation will be engaged by a practice like organizing only when it is deeply rooted in the institution's spiritual life.

A teaching handbook on the "hallmarks of an organized church" produced by CTC and Citizens UK describes the integration of theology, spirituality, and action in more detail: "The congregation will see the reality celebrated in their liturgy as deeply connected with their community-building during the week. The liturgy will truly be the work of the whole people of God. They will pray for public concerns and celebrate public victories in their worship. The teaching and prayer ministries of the church will help church members integrate doctrine, prayer and practice in their daily lives—so that public action takes its rightful place as part of a holistic understanding of the mission of the Church and the vocation of each Christian."[41] The focus here is deliberately on the spiritual life of the *whole* congregation, not just a small cadre of activists.

Pope Francis's ministry shows how to focus on popular rather than merely activist spirituality. In his time as archbishop of Buenos Aires, he experienced conflict with progressive Catholic activists because his interest was in the spirituality of the poor, not just that of activists who sought to agitate on their behalf. As the pope's biographer Austin Ivereigh observes, this is "what happens in a diocese whose bishop takes seriously the preferential option for the poor." Progressive Catholics complained that under Archbishop Bergoglio (as he then was) "popular devotion has become the paradigmatic piety." The assumption made by the progressives was that "the poor need to be weaned off their pre-modern religiosity, not indulged by their archbishop."[42]

As Rafael Luciani explains, Francis's approach (both as archbishop and now as pope) draws on the *teología del pueblo* that has developed in the Latin American church. This theology regards the poorest "not merely as the objects of liberation or education, but as individuals capable of living the faith legitimately in their own manner, capable of forging paths based on their own culture." While they are sometimes dismissed as uncultured, in reality their culture is simply "one that differs from that of the middle class."[43] Luciani notes that this approach has generated opposition and that "some even regard it as populist"—including, rather tellingly, "persons who, while they are concerned about the situation of the poor today, have never dealt personally with them or shared their lives."[44]

There is, as it were, a "spiritual populism" that corresponds to the wider populism of the organizing movement. At its most authentic, community organizing in churches echoes Bergoglio's approach in its confidence that the Holy Spirit speaks to the whole of God's people, not merely to an educated or clerical elite. For Pope Francis, "popular devotion" did not imply a laissez-faire attitude toward theological orthodoxy. If anything, the poorest worshipers in Buenos Aires were likely to be more theologically conservative than their middle-class critics.

The study of Scripture is central to how both Christians and Muslims in East London understand their prayer lives and their social action. This point is exemplified by the campaign for a Community Land Trust in Shadwell. To date, this has been London Citizens' most successful neighborhood campaign for affordable housing. In June 2016, a "walk for affordable housing" identified a piece of land owned by Transport for London (an agency of the Greater London Authority) that would be suitable for a Community Land Trust. By January 2018 it had secured the site, winning affordable homes for around 140 local people. The team leading the campaign was largely drawn from St. George-in-the-East (a Church of England parish) and a group of local Muslim women who met regularly to study the Qur'an in local homes.

Similarly, St. George's involvement in the affordable housing campaign grew out of a wider process of congregational renewal through community organizing, in which a deepening of the church's life of prayer and Bible study played a central role.[45] One of the fruits of this study was the rediscovery of the Biblical imperative to engage with and learn from those beyond the church's walls.

In many churches there is a fear that engaging with "the Other" will inevitably compromise the integrity of the institution's faithfulness to Christ. However, the experience of churches engaged in organizing is that the practice can intensify that faithfulness. As the congregation at St. George's discovered, Jesus encourages his disciples to be open to the insights of those beyond the existing community of faith. (This is the key, and often overlooked, message of the Parable of the Good Samaritan—not that Jesus's hearers are called to be "Good Samaritans" but rather that generosity and faithfulness to God are being exemplified by someone outside their community.) As one member of the group observed—reflecting on both her study of the Bible and her experience of organizing—"My Muslim neighbors are teaching me to be a better Christian!"

Engagement with community organizing in fact calls Christians to a practice *more* consonant with Jesus's own teaching in two particular areas—his use of tension and his positive estimation of power. This is an area in which the Christian experience of organizing is echoed in Muslim and Jewish engagement. The Scriptures of all three faiths summon their readers to confront systemic injustice. However, there is a constant temptation for churches, mosques, and synagogues alike to focus on the safer territory of acts of charity (which can preserve, and even entrench, existing inequalities of power) and to avoid the more difficult internal and external tensions generated by challenging injustice and redistributing power.

In summary, Bachelard's challenge is an important and illuminating one. The experience of Christians, Muslims, and Jews in London Citizens suggests that a deep engagement with organizing must move beyond the "functional atheism" in which their ethical convictions become detached from the wider spiritual lives of their institutions. The experience of Christians and Muslims involved in the Shadwell housing campaign is that, when organizing became integrated into their wider life of prayer and Scriptural reflection, the journey beyond the walls of their own faith community helped them to become *more* faithful to its teachings rather than watering those teachings down.

"WEDGE" ISSUES

In building a broad-based alliance Alinsky avoided campaigning on what he called the "wedge" issues—issues that divided people in the poorest neighborhoods from one another. While people's organizations sought to generate tension with those *beyond* the alliances, it was axiomatic that action would be taken only on issues on which the interests and beliefs of diverse groups led to a common desire for action. Issues on which those groups could not agree were left to one side.

This has remained central to the approach of both IAF and Citizens UK. For the diverse range of institutions that participate, it offers a certain kind of security. Muslims and Christians, Jews and Secular Humanists can all participate in the knowledge that they will not be outvoted and forced to sign on to a campaign platform that goes against their convictions. As we saw in the case of the anti-usury campaign, there may be a need for pragmatic compromises, but the aim of the process of deliberation within Citizens UK is consensus: Each campaign has the active support of the full range of worldviews brought together in its pluralist alliance.

While this process ensures that no institution is asked to campaign *against* its core beliefs, one obvious objection remains. If *all* of an institution's public action is taken in alliance with others, will that not involve its downplaying the controversial aspects of its belief system?

Abortion is an obvious case in point. Citizens UK and IAF bring churches involved in campaigns against abortion together with trade unions and student unions that actively support campaigns to widen legal access to abortion. For the alliance, abortion is therefore a wedge issue. However, engaging in organizing does not in any way limit the capacity of an institution to engage (outside of the organizing process) in campaigns on opposing sides of this issue.

Each institution will need to discern how much of its energy it will put into the campaigns in which it can make common cause with others—and how much to focus on wedge issues. While the paid organizers in Citizens UK and IAF will obviously want to maximize institutional engagement in the former set of issues, it is important that they respect an institution's discernment of its priorities and avoid speaking in a way that suggests that the former set of issues (those around which a consensus can be reached) is more important. There is no neutral vantage point from which to evaluate the relative importance of these different issues. For religious and nonreligious institutions alike, that discernment is necessarily an internal matter.

Community organizing is therefore only one of the practices necessary if negotiated pluralism is to succeed. In chapter 1 I outlined three kinds of conversation that are necessary in a pluralist context: mutual witness, negotiation, and debate. The practice of organizing facilitates only the first two of these. However, there are two ways in which it can make an indirect contribution to the quality of debate that takes place on wedge issues. Most obviously, the weaving of trust and solidarity between people on the issues on which they can make common cause creates a far more fruitful space for engagement on the issues on which deep disagreement remains. It is far harder to parody and stereotype an opponent on an issue such as abortion if one has come to know the same person as an ally in the struggle for a living wage, say. The experience of common action need not in any way dilute the strength of one's convictions on the issue about which there is disagreement. Nor need it reduce one's estimation of the importance of this wedge issue. But it creates the possibility of a different tone for the engagement.

Moreover, many of the hallmarks of organizing—building relationships across difference, discerning the self-interest of others, and developing leaders and redistributing power within one's organization—are practices that can inform an institution's campaigning even on wedge issues.

For example, those Christians who campaign for restrictions on access to abortion persistently rely on a disproportionate number of male figures to defend their position. This leads to an understandable perception that the position involves "men seeking to impose their moral positions on women's bodies." The polling evidence suggests a more nuanced position: In the United Kingdom at least, women are significantly more likely to hold a conservative position on the issue. As the (pro-abortion) *Guardian* reported: "Polls consistently show . . . that women are more likely than men to support a reduction on the abortion limit. In the 2011 YouGov poll 28% of men supported a reduction, 46% of women did. In the 2012 YouGov poll 24% of men supported a reduction, 49% of women did. In the Angus Reid poll 35% of men supported a reduction in the limit, 59% of women did. In the ICM poll 45% of men supported a reduction to 20 weeks, 59% of women did."[46]

In the United Kingcom, the dominance of male voices in the Church is thus obscuring a crucial fact that would address an important criticism of the anti-abortion position. Thus, the redistribution of power within the Church—which Pope Francis has identified as an important priority, both with respect to gender and more generally[47]—would help the many Christians who wish to make a case to the wider society for less relaxed abortion laws. It would enable the "pro-life" position to be understood not as a matter of one gender "imposing its morals" on the bodies of another, but as one in which a very significant number of *women* feel that the fetus (either from conception or at a later stage in the womb) is a life whose value also needs to be protected more fully in legislation.

In the American context, by contrast, the Pew Institute has found "no significant gender differences in views of whether abortion should be legal."[48] In the United States, as in the United Kingdom, the failure to give prominence to women's voices within the Church has allowed a narrative to develop that effectively ignores the significant number of women who would favor a less relaxed abortion policy.

The point of this illustration is not to align the community organizing movement with either a pro-life or a pro-choice position. Both IAF and Citizens UK have member institutions with diametrically opposed views on abortion and are therefore careful not to take any collective position on such a divisive issue. My argument on abortion is twofold, and each part applies to wedge issues more generally. First, organizing can help to create more constructive dialogues between those who hold very different positions. Second, when one side is willing to attend respectfully to the genuine concerns of its opponents, it may be possible to make a more compelling case without compromising its core beliefs.

CONCLUSION

In chapters 1 and 2 I presented a general case for inclusive populism and argued that community organizing embodies such a populism. In this chapter, I have addressed six criticisms of organizing, three of which question its desirability and a further three of which question its impact. I have defended the practice against all three of the criticisms of its desirability, showing the value of some of its most controversial features—its populism, its refusal of progressive tests, and its focus on self-interest—and their inextricable relationship to the goods that organizing generates.

The challenges to organizing's impact needed a more nuanced response. The claim that organizing has been tried and has failed—whether in the Obama presidency or in the Big Society program of David Cameron—does not stand up to scrutiny. But it does raise important questions as to the relationship between organizing and the vocation of politicians. Far from seeking to supersede elective politics, community organizing can help to create an environment in which such politics can flourish.

Perhaps unsurprisingly, the practice of organizing does not always live up to its rhetoric. That is true of all political processes. What is distinctive about organizing is its self-correcting nature, embodied in the maxim that "all organizing is reorganizing." The authenticity of organizing's populism depends on the faithful, patient application of this principle, for it builds powerful and lasting alliances for change.

When the teachings of organizing are applied in this patient, faithful way, it is able to embody a genuine pluralism. Over-hasty organizing is ultimately ineffective. The real danger is not that inner-city evangelical churches, Catholic parishes, or Islamic centers will somehow be corralled into subscribing to an alien set of values. Rather, when organizing fails to attend to the beliefs, values (and, in most cases, the spiritualities), of these different institutions, their engagement with the alliance remains superficial. Only when organizing is patient and gives each institution time to discern the rationale for engagement is an alliance built that will be politically effective precisely because it is truly owned by its diverse institutions.

CHAPTER 5

Integration, Islam, and Immigration

Anxiety about immigration and integration—and in particular about the integration of Muslim immigrants—has been a key factor in the rise of right-wing populism. In this chapter I consider the light community organizing casts on these issues.

I have argued that our current political crisis is due in part to the top-down approach of political liberalism. To address it, there needs to be a transformation in the *process* of politics, not just a revision of the policies it generates. My approach to these the issues of integration in general, the integration of Muslims in particular, and immigration reflects this conviction. In each case, community organizing does not simply generate alternative policies. It begins with a transformation of political processes. This will, in turn, generate more fruitful policies, as well as a political context in which they are more likely to succeed.

INTEGRATION

Like many parents, I used to take my eldest son to a local nursery. In the reception area there was a large, laminated Union Jack. On it was written an explanation of how the nursery "promotes British values." The values listed were "democracy, the rule of law, individual liberty, mutual respect, and tolerance of those with different faiths and beliefs." In the past few years, such displays have sprung up in a variety of educational and social settings in response to legislation initiated by Education Secretary Michael Gove in 2014 to tackle extremism and promote integration.

Aside from its rather hectoring tone, two things struck me about this curious display. First, putting up such notices did not seem a very British thing to do. Ironically, it was Michael Gove who best articulated my unease. When asked to define "British values" back in 2007, he replied, "There is something rather un-British about seeking to define British-ness."[1] Secondly, the values listed seemed rather abstract. They might be democratic values, but it was hard to see what makes them distinctively British. The laminated Union Jack seemed rather redundant: Surely the same words could appear in front of a French or Irish tricolor, the stars and stripes of the United States, or the six-colored flag of the new South Africa.

As Shamit Saggar and Will Somerville explain, Gove's 2014 legislation is symptomatic of a wider shift in integration policy toward what they term "liberal coercion":

> The government's approach to integration has changed substantially since the mid-1990s, with the emphasis shifting toward increasing the obligations on new, first-generation immigrants to integrate (for example, a language examination and citizenship test were introduced in 2004). . . . Significant changes can be inferred from new integration programs for refugees; new citizenship classes, testing, and ceremonies; pre-departure language testing; and efforts to promote community cohesion. They can also be seen in the introduction of a points-based system to assess immigrants' potential utility for the UK economy and that favors specific labor-market needs.[2]

Such a coercive policy emerges as a direct consequence of political liberalism. As I showed in chapter 1, liberalism rejects the use of elective politics to discern and pursue a common good. On its conception of politics, the role of the state is purely functional: to enable diverse communities, with differing interests and differing moral frameworks, to live together in peace. Precisely because liberalism seeks to keep specific conceptions of the good out of political discourse, its version of "British values" can only be a set of fairly abstract universals that float free from specific, embedded relationships and from any substantive moral vision. In consequence, integration policy develops a coercive aspect. It will have to police the adherence of diverse ethnic and religious groups to a set of abstract "values" they have had little or no role in formulating. Not surprisingly, this leads to politicians' being experienced as hectoring and superior, for the dominant mode of integration policy is telling citizens how they ought to behave. Host communities are told they need to be more tolerant of those with different faiths and beliefs; those who are arriving are told they need to be more willing to integrate.

In order to devise a more effective integration policy, there must be a re-conception of the process by which national values develop. As I argue below, this will lead to a transformation of the process by which citizens (whether new migrants or established communities) develop a sense of loyalty toward those values.

NEGOTIATED PLURALISM AND NATIONAL VALUES

Negotiated pluralism offers a very different account of the way in which "national values" emerge. Its focus is not on abstract norms but on concrete relationships, that is, on the ways in which citizens, in particular times and places, seek to build a common life and discern a common good. Former archbishop of Canterbury Rowan Williams argues that the language of "British values" makes sense only in such a narrative form:

> There is no useful way of talking about "British-ness" without telling a specific story—a story which is about how both invasion and foreign adventure created a flexible and hybrid language, how a particular kind of concordat between royal, feudal and ecclesiastical power outlasted a brief experiment with royal absolutism in the early modern period, how the reaction against absolutism moulded a set of legal standards and protocols (habeas corpus, jury trial), how lessons were learned and not learned in the treatment of subject societies through England's relations with its Celtic neighbors . . . and so on.[3]

To speak of national values, then, is to recount how a particular set of people have built a common life and negotiated their differing conceptions of the good. Such a narrative need not be triumphalist. Indeed, honesty and repentance are key parts of any healthy national story.

Each nation's narrative is still unfolding. As Williams observes, a variant of the liberal mistake is the assumption "that constructive historical conflict and negotiation are essentially over, and that there is now a self-evident state of political rationality prevailing, which lays down clear and universal principles for social stability and equity." This mistaken assumption will also lead to liberal coercion, as if integration policy simply consisted in ensuring compliance with these "clear and universal principles" rather than the inclusion of new citizens in an ongoing conversation.

To think of national values as the product of a continuing conversation is not to embrace moral relativism. The "conversation" in question is one between citizens who hold diverse beliefs but who are engaged in a process of discerning together what is genuinely beautiful, good, and true. This is not a purely, or even primarily, cerebral process: Citizens of a nation-state seek to discern what is good as they build a common life in relationships with other people and institutions in their neighborhoods.

This re-conception of national values leads to a very different understanding of integration. Rather than being a matter of subscribing to a set of "clear and universal principles" specified by the state, integration involves a willingness to enter into an ongoing conversation. Such a conversation is, of course, easier to recommend than it is to actually design. Precisely because "realities are greater than ideas," integration policy requires attentiveness to the concrete practices that will build solidarity and trust between different communities.

The ongoing nature of the conversation is also important if "integration" is not to be a way in which those in power resist challenges to the status quo. As the Commission on Religion and Belief in British Public Life (CoRAB) observes, "It is important to recognize and address the ambiguity of the concept of integration." CoRAB continues: "Religion and belief have often inspired a critique of the existing state of a society. The work of William and Catherine Booth—exposing and challenging the exploitation of workers (and in particular children) in Victorian London—is one of many examples of religion and belief disturbing and challenging the status quo. The demand to integrate must not be allowed to silence the prophetic and disturbing voices of those who challenge injustice."[4] Like the language of "integration," the language of "religious extremism" can be used to silence challenges to the status quo. As Archbishop of Canterbury Justin Welby observed, according to the definition of some government ministers, any faithful Christian would count as an extremist because "we do not believe as Christians that the rule of law outweighs everything else, we believe that the kingdom of God outweighs everything else."[5] Welby's point was reinforced by research carried out by opinion pollsters ComRes for the United Kingdom's Evangelical Alliance, which showed that 28 percent of Britons considered Jesus Christ an extremist. Other religious figures deemed "extremist" were the Dalai Lama (13 percent), Mahatma Gandhi (20 percent), and Martin Luther King Jr. and Nelson Mandela (25 percent each).[6] The danger identified by CoRAB is not an abstract one: There is a genuine risk that the liberal coercion at the heart of UK integration policy serves to entrench established hierarchies of power and stifle peaceful discussion of radical alternatives.

As we have seen, the approach of community organizing is to begin with the self-interest and lived experiences of the different groups that share a common space. Organizing has a focus on institutions as well as individuals and groups, for institutions are keepers of a corporate memory and the means by which citizens articulate a common story. By understanding the experiences of different communities and engaging with their institutions, organizing seeks to weave relationships of trust and solidarity instead of seeking to force "integration" through top-down coercion.

The next two sections present case studies from inner-city London—one of a community of recent migrants dispersed across the city and the other of a working-class community concentrated in a particular place. These case studies demonstrate how the practice of organizing generates the kind of integration that liberal coercion has proved unable to achieve. After considering the parallels and differences with the US context, I will seek to draw out some implications for integration policy in both countries.

LONDON'S CONGOLESE DIASPORA

The Congolese community is a particularly challenging one for community organizing, as it is for top-down integration policies. Most Congolese migrants are fairly recent arrivals. They come from a non-Commonwealth country in which English is usually a third or fourth language. Moreover, the continuing traumas of war in their homeland mean that such energy as migrants have for civic and political engagement is often focused outside the United Kingdom. These factors are rarely taken into account in the public debate about the importance of integration. It is deeply un-helpful to offer migrants lectures about the need to integrate, particularly when those issuing such strictures lack any understanding of why those migrants' experiences make such integration more difficult.

The approach of Citizens UK offers a sharp contrast to top-down integration policy. Rather than setting a priori standards of "good in-tegration" that all migrants should meet, the movement has sought to understand the existing needs and priorities of specific diaspora commu-nities (their self-interest) and to discern the areas in which theirs overlap with those of other groups. To achieve this, the alliance formed the New Citizens Organizing Team (NCOT). This enables diaspora groups to ad-dress issues specific to those communities, notably immigration and child detention. One of the most prominent recent outcomes of this agenda has been the New Citizens Legal Service, described here:

> A huge challenge for people seeking status in the UK is negotiating a
> highly complex immigration system. There is little guidance from the
> UK Border Agency on how to work through the system; as a result,
> people frequently turn for help to members of their own community.
> However, this process is often exploitative. Numerous cases of fraud
> and exploitation were unveiled through Citizens UK's listening pro-
> cess. On many occasions those seeking legal status were given false or
> inaccurate legal advice by "cowboy" solicitors at vast expense. To ad-
> dress this problem, Citizens UK developed an innovative triaging pro-
> cess by which quality professional solicitors from a number of leading
> firms would work on a pro bono basis to provide legal and reliable
> immigration signposting. Through this process the alliance could en-
> sure that members of Diaspora communities were aware of their sta-
> tus and the steps they needed to take to negotiate the system without
> being taken advantage of.[7]

Many of the issues identified in diaspora organizing are ones on which common cause can be made with the wider neighborhood-based alliance. Moreover, the process of organizing itself (the one-to-one meet-ings and the sharing of stories) has gradually helped new migrants as well as more established communities to understand one another's perspec-tives and to have greater empathy for the differences in the ways they en-gage in the public square.

As part of our research, Caitlin Burbridge conducted interviews with members of London's Congolese diaspora involved in community organizing. The key obstacles to integration identified by her research are migrants' attachment to their home country rather than to their new neighborhood and city; experiences of exclusion in the new context; linguistic and cultural barriers; and differing conceptions of civil society.[8]

The first of these factors (the attachment of diaspora groups to their home countries) is already well researched. Different diaspora communities have experiences that intensify or reduce this attachment. Inevitably this has an impact on the extent to which migrants desire to participate in civic life in their new context.

In Burbridge's interviews with members of the Congolese diaspora, physical and verbal abuse was repeatedly mentioned as a factor compounding their sense of isolation. Inevitably the experience of physical and racial abuse amplifies fear across the well-established social networks of such small diaspora communities.

Burbridge's research also identifies particular linguistic and cultural barriers to inclusion. Congolese migrants who had not been through specific English language training found it difficult to participate in discussions with members of other member institutions within Citizens UK. These linguistic barriers reinforced other obstacles. "When it is only [one or two key] leaders who speak English and can listen to the community to relay the issues that they face to an organizer" Burbridge recounts, "there is only so much influence an organizer can have in terms of ensuring the development of a range of leaders who are articulating the needs of the breadth of the community—making it very difficult to achieve change, regardless of how many lay people want to be involved."[9]

Finally, differing notions of civil society are often at play in diaspora communities. The prior understandings migrants bring of the relationship between the state and civil society in their country of origin and the processes by which change is achieved in that context shape their expectations of how such processes are likely to work in their new context. As Burbridge explains: "Having experienced power being asserted through predominantly violent means, conceptualizing the effectiveness of state accountability through processes of negotiation and non-violent action requires a significant shift in mind-set. Community organizing does recognize the need to unlearn power structures in order to re-learn new ones. However, the principle of unlearning structures and re-learning structures requires more than just a change in knowledge base. This process requires a long-term commitment to engaging people in evolving democratic processes, and recognizing that this will take time."[10] While Burbridge's research identifies a particular set of challenges in relation to new diaspora communities, it also provides evidence that patient engagement with the realities of their self-interest can build relationships between new migrants and the wider culture that will help them to integrate successfully.

Engagement with the existing interests of the individuals and institutions of new diaspora communities has led to some distinctive organizing initiatives, such as the New Citizens Legal Service. It has also identified areas for action so that new migrants can organize alongside other communities. In the Congolese community, concerns about physical safety led to involvement in Citizens UK's "CitySafe" campaign.

CitySafe grew out of the response of South Londoners to the murder of teenager Jimmy Mizen. His parents, Barry and Margaret, became leading figures in the campaign to recruit shops, libraries, and other local institutions as "CitySafe Havens." Staff in these organizations received special training and agreed to display signs indicating that their organizations were havens. People who felt insecure (particularly teenagers being threatened by violent gangs) could then slip into a designated "Haven," where staff would decide whether to accompany them home or to call the police. As Yvette's story shows, the CitySafe campaign meant that the physical abuse her son faced did not isolate her from the wider community but inspired her to organize with non-Congolese neighbors around their common interest in neighborhood safety.

Yvette is the mother to four children. Her eldest, Jeremy, attends a school in a different borough than the one where they live. Yvette entered the United Kingdom as an economic migrant, unlike many of the other chaplaincy members. Her greatest fear has been for the safety of her son. Jeremy gets a bus to school and talks of being bullied both physically and verbally because of his race. Yvette talks of a time when Jeremy was severely beaten and abandoned on the top deck of a bus. No one else on the bus came to help him. Jeremy's story is not isolated. Stories like this not only are problematic for those who experience such direct abuse but they also intensify a sense of inferiority or insecurity in the wider diaspora community. The community organizing response to such stories has been to launch the "CitySafe

Campaign." This offers a way in which those who experience violence (inflicted either on them directly or on a close relative or friend) can take practical action to make their neighborhood safer.[11]

The experience of the Congolese diaspora is echoed in other communities in which Citizens UK practices community organizing. After a process of listening to and engaging low-paid workers in and around its parish (which lies on the edge of London's main financial district) St. George-in-the-East launched English, Prayer, Action, a congregation set up to respond to the practical and spiritual needs of workers for whom English is a second language, many of whom are unable to attend church on Sundays due to shift work. The focus was initially on the immediate self-interests of low-paid workers (drawn mainly from the Brazilian diaspora), which were to learn English to reduce their isolation, improve their economic prospects, and address bullying in the workplace. Through patient attention to their existing concerns, parishioners have gradually identified areas of common concern between them and the migrants. Existing Citizens UK campaigns to address the behavior of rogue landlords and to secure affordable housing speak to the concerns and aspirations of low-paid workers and may form the basis for common action in the years ahead.

As each of these examples shows, a desire for "integration" cannot be imposed by Government fiat. Most new migrants are consumed with the challenges of survival. They are struggling to earn a living and raise a family in an alien context in which they have little grasp of English. They may also be contending with racism, workplace bullying, and predatory landlords and immigration lawyers. When those daily struggles are shared within the ambit of the organizing process, common interests emerge. Only then do the trust and solidarity that are essential to genuine integration begin to emerge.

BARKING AND DAGENHAM

The stories of the Congolese and Brazilian diaspora indicate the inadequacy of "liberal coercion" as a policy toward migrants; the policy is equally inadequate in its treatment of Britain's established working-class communities. Research in the London Borough of Barking and Dagenham illustrates this point.

White working-class discontent—around both economic status and recent inflows of migration—were significant factors in President Trump's election victory. In the United Kingdom, similar factors were at work in the Brexit victory in the 2016 referendum on European Union membership. As I have argued elsewhere, these two phenomena should not be equated.[12] While it would be impossible to embrace inclusive populism and simultaneously support the rhetoric and policies of the Trump administration, many who would agree with the analysis in this book are also firmly committed to Britain's departure from the EU.[13] For all that, it is clear that one of the key constituencies supporting Brexit was white, working-class voters angered by the impact of the global financial crash on their economic well-being. This group linked their economic woes to policies facilitating immigration to the United Kingdom.

Moreover, the surge in hate crimes against ethnic minorities (including white Eastern Europeans) and Muslims in the aftermath of the EU referendum result indicates a significant degree of hostility from a section of white Britons. The rise of the overtly racist British National Party (BNP) in the early 2000s was an earlier indication of this sentiment. The BNP secured twelve of the thirteen seats it contested on the Barking and Dagenham Council in 2006 and then won almost one million votes in the 2009 European Election. The subsequent collapse of the BNP did not signify the disappearance of such attitudes. Rather, these voters were attracted to more mainstream parties (most notably the United Kingdom Independence Party) that also opposed EU membership and further large-scale immigration. In 2016, Barking and Dagenham was one of the five London boroughs (out of thirty-three) where a majority voted to leave the EU.

In the aftermath of the Brexit vote, community organizers Sotez Chowdhury and Dan Firth began research on the attitudes of the white working-class communities at the heart of the Brexit vote.[14] Chowdhury's interviews, focus groups, and community interviews in Barking and Dagenham provide insight into the experience of some of London's poorest white voters. As he told me, "A significant number of the white working class members of our focus group did openly say xenophobic and racist things. However, after a little probing we discovered a more complex picture." People felt their communities had started changing in the 1980s as the social housing stock was depleted through the "Right to Buy" policy of the Conservative government. In the memories of these residents, tensions with these wealthier white "incomers" predated the tensions and resentments about more recent immigration flows (from the Horn of Africa, the Congo, and Eastern Europe). Across these two major changes—the influx caused by "Right to Buy" and the later arrival of many immigrants—there was a real feeling of loss of community. According to many long-standing residents, "It went from us knowing everybody to us knowing nobody." There was a feeling of alienation from both economic and political power: "They don't cater for us" was a lament that ran across the comments on shops and cafes, council services, jobs, and housing.

These changes affected the quality of life of long-term residents in a number of other ways. Recent immigrants often lived in overcrowded housing, a situation leading to piles of rubbish, noise, and tension. And whereas jobs had historically been plentiful and secure, they were now scarce, low-paid, and insecure. As Chowdhury observes, these last two complaints reveal problems that immigrants and long-standing residents in fact share: "Many of the underlying issues for both immigrants and long-time residents have to do with the lack of secure jobs and decent, affordable housing, and with a long-term failure of existing political structures to engage or represent them. This results in tensions between communities that are suffering the same issues. This same theme is found in other [Brexit-voting] towns like Bilston (Black Country) or Boston (Lincolnshire), which were former manufacturing or agricultural areas that offered many jobs."[15] At the time of this writing, the first churches, mosques, and schools are joining TELCO in Barking and Dagenham. One of the particular challenges of organizing in white working-class communities is that usually a lower proportion of residents are involved in voluntary associations than in most migrant communities, in which religious institutions and cultural associations remain vibrant. Schools are a particularly important part of the alliance if it is to reach communities in which fewer residents engage in voluntary associations, for they can be effective at engaging parents as well as children. The IAF's "Alliance Schools" program in the United States shows the potential of this work. In East London we have found that churches and mosques can play an important role in engaging local schools.

As in the case of the Congolese diaspora, the key to successful organizing is to begin with existing interests and then begin to identify and act on common concerns. It is striking how many of the concerns identified by Chowdhury in Barking and Dagenham correspond to issues on which

TELCO has taken action in these other East London boroughs through campaigns for "Jobs with Dignity," the Living Wage, and affordable housing (through Community Land Trusts and a Living Rent).

My own ministry in East London bears this out. Tower Hamlets has a particular history of intercommunal tension around housing allocation. The experience of churches, mosques, and schools organizing together for affordable homes has changed the attitudes of a number of white and Afro-Caribbean residents toward their Bengali neighbors, however, moving these groups from rivals fighting over a dwindling supply of affordable homes to colleagues joining together to secure more such housing. Even long-standing residents who have worked in multi-racial churches and organized across faiths have come to an appreciation of the actual life experiences of migrants previously seen only through the lens of hostile media coverage. When people develop trust and solidarity through action on the issues they already care about, they begin to discover more, and care more, about the situations of those with whom they are working.

In London, community organizing is engaging an increasing diversity of individuals and institutions—Muslims working alongside Evangelical, Pentecostal, and Catholic Christians as well as secular trade unionists. Across the city, organizing is drawing often isolated diaspora communities into engagement with other groups. Its success flows from a willingness to engage with each group as it is rather than setting *a priori* demands as to what they ought to care about.

INTEGRATION IN THE UNITED STATES

A British observer of the 2016 US presidential election would have noticed significant similarities to the British context. Indeed, the Trump campaign repeatedly claimed that the Brexit vote was a sign that its anti-establishment "populism" was part of a global revolt against "liberal elites." Nigel Farage, the leader of the UK Independence Party and a key figure in the Brexit campaign, appeared at Trump rallies and emphasized these synergies. In particular, Trump and Farage claimed that the livelihoods and lifestyles of existing working-class communities were being threatened by immigration. Politicians in both the United Kingdom and the United States campaigns stoked fears of Muslim immigrants alongside attacks on the wider flow of migrants (in the United Kingdom, from Eastern Europe and in the United States, from Latin America).

The most profound difference in the US context was the position of its African American citizens. In 1951 the total Black, Asian, and Minority Ethnic (BAME) population in England and Wales was around 103,000, that is, around 2 percent of the population.[16] By contrast, the 1950 US census records a BAME population of over 13 million—around 10 percent of the total. To frame issues of integration and multiculturalism in the United States in terms of immigration alone is to render the African American population invisible and to overlook the legacy of slavery. Yet this is precisely how Trump and "white nationalists" such as Steve Bannon choose to frame the debate. Trump's campaign was fueled by racist animus, but the animus was expressed differently across communities. Explicit hostility was shown to Latin American immigrants: Trump claimed a Mexican American judge would inevitably be biased against him, nicknamed Senator Elizabeth Warren "Pocahontas" because of her claims of a mixed-race heritage, and attacked all Mexican immigrants as "rapists and drug users." A similar animus was directed against Muslims. Trump's hostility toward African Americans was (at least before the election) expressed in a more oblique, deniable way—by attacking the Black Lives Matter campaign, questioning Obama's ancestry, and implying that he was a closet Muslim.

One reason for this is clear: The history of slavery and segregation is incompatible with the myth of a self-sufficient white nation besieged by hostile nonwhite economic migrants. Whereas focusing on Hispanics and Muslims creates the impression that pluralism is a recent issue generated by immigration, the story of African Americans shows that pluralism was a founding reality of American history.

The racial diversity at the heart of American history comes from the people who occupied the land prior to the arrival of the white population and from the Africans whom white people brought with them or subsequently enslaved. To acknowledge that complex racial history is to reframe questions of immigration and integration in a way far less amenable to the distorted narratives favored by right-wing populism, for it undermines the white "us" versus the nonwhite "them" dichotomy at the heart of Trumpian populism.

The surge in far-right populism makes the challenge of integration—building a common life and discerning a common good—particularly urgent in today's United States. The Trump victory has led to an intense debate among progressive commentators on its causes, and thus on the most effective response. Mark Lilla argues that progressive identity politics has made it impossible for the left to build an election-winning coalition. In particular, he claims that identity politics has alienated the white working class. Aspects of Lilla's analysis clearly ring true: "Today's activists and leaders are formed almost exclusively in our colleges and universities, as members of the mainly liberal professions of law, journalism and education. Liberal political education now takes place, if it takes place at all, on campuses that are detached socially and geographically from the sorts of people who once were the foundation of the Democratic Party."[17] In a striking echo of Hillary Clinton's rejection of community organizing, Lilla's preference is for political parties over social movements because, he maintains, "over the long term [social movements] are incapable of achieving any concrete political ends on their own. They need system politicians and public officials sympathetic to the movement aims but willing to engage in the slow, patient work of campaigning for office, drawing up legislation, making trades to get it passed, and then overseeing bureaucracies to get it enforced."[18]

Like Tony Blair's, however, Lilla's critique remains within a liberal frame. He is calling for a more effective "liberal fight-back" rather than a fundamental re-examination of the liberal political project. This solution is inadequate given the scale of the problem and the structural weaknesses of liberalism.

Lilla dismisses community organizing in a sentence (as a mere "vestige of the New Left"). In a telling section, he shows no understanding of the practice. He claims that "social movements" are necessarily "centrifugal, encouraging splits into smaller and smaller factions obsessed with single issues." By contrast, "healthy political parties" are "centripedal" and "encourage factions and interests to come together to work out common goals and strategies."[19] He makes these assertions without any reference to empirical research. As we have seen, there is already an extensive literature demonstrating that community organizing is an effective process for engaging diverse interest groups to "work out common goals and strategies."

The work of IAF demonstrates that the interests of African Americans, Latino migrants, and the white working class are not a zero-sum game. It also shows that a practice that begins with their distinct interests and institutions can bring these diverse citizens together. The movement's work in New Orleans in the wake of Hurricane Katrina was a case in point. Jeffrey Stout tells the story of the local organizing alliance (called Jeremiah) in *Blessed Are the Organized*. In the words of Jeremiah's one paid organizer, the evacuation after the hurricane led the city's elites to imagine that they "had a clean slate to work with. . . . All the things dreamed about in the deepest darkest secrets of their minds were now possible." This was an opportunity to reduce the population, making New Orleans a "wealthier, whiter" place. Stout describes the response of the citizens who faced displacement:

> A delicate balance needs to be struck if a multiracial coalition is to be constructed in post-Katrina New Orleans. Jeremiah leaders are taking four steps to achieve that balance. First, they are carefully distinguishing racial identification from being concerned about racism and its effects. Second, they are trying to explain in clear and accessible language how racial factors combined with economic factors to bring about the crisis they face. Third, Jeremiah is trying to show all groups, including corporate executives and the residents of Metairie [a New Orleans suburb], how their interests would be served by joining the coalition. And fourth, Jeremiah is trying to articulate a vision of a common good in which those interests converge.[20]

The Jeremiah alliance's response neither obscures the realities of historic oppression and contemporary racism nor allows those realities to have the last word in the lives of its people. They show how integration can truly be accomplished.

RETHINKING INTEGRATION POLICY

What implications does all this have for policy-makers charged with the formulation of integration policy? In their treatment of new migrants, policy-makers need to acknowledge the challenges the first generation faces in building a life in a new country by engaging with new institutions and establishing their own civil society organizations. Dilowar Khan's story in chapter 2 shows how these can be complementary goals. It is precisely because their neighbors in TELCO fought for land for the London Muslim Centre that members of East London Mosque built deep relationships with them over the twenty years that followed—relationships that, more recently, have inspired many other mosques from across the capital to follow them into membership in a community organizing alliance. The same point is made by Cailtin Burbridge's research: Establishing a distinct stream of organizing work to engage with diaspora communities has not isolated new migrants from the rest of London Citizens' members but rather provided a more effective pathway into that wider alliance.

The experience of the United States shows that "integration policy" is not the most important government policy affecting integration. As Tomás Jiménez explains:

> The strategy that has dominated the approach to immigrant integration in the United States since the 1920s can best be described as laissez faire. Rather than relying on an organized and unified governmental strategy, this laissez faire approach depends on a combination of immigrants' motivation, economic expansion, and a robust public education system to achieve integration. As immigrants and their descendants receive better jobs, move to more affluent neighborhoods, join the military, and attend college and graduate school, they find themselves interacting with members of other ethnoracial and national-origin groups in such a way that social boundaries based on race, class, and religion diminish.[21]

While there may be a role for a more proactive integration policy in the United States, the primary focus of policy-makers should not be on initiatives to promote "national values" or even "social cohesion." More important are the wider economic issues—access to work, public services, and affordable housing—that emerge from both new migrants and settled residents in community organizing listening campaigns. Indeed, on both sides of the Atlantic, truly effective "integration policies" must address housing, wages, and jobs—issues that emerge out of an authentic engagement with the daily experiences of the communities they seek to bring together.

ISLAM AND INTEGRATION

While resentment against immigrants *in general* has fueled the rise of far-right populism, there has been a particular animus against Muslim migrants. As we saw in chapter 1, the arrival of significant numbers of

Muslim immigrants in the United Kingdom has posed particular challenges to a liberal political framework because their religious identity is so evidently lived out in the public sphere as well as in private devotion. As CoRAB has argued, religious identities are entwined with ethnic and cultural identities: "Most people reading this report probably see their approach to religion and belief as a consequence of their personal decision. However, it has always been the case, in Britain as throughout the world, that for some people, in certain locations and circumstances and at certain times and in certain respects, religion is not only a matter of personal deliberation, choice and commitment. Rather, it can be determined—partly, largely or even entirely—by the family and community into which a person is born, and by how they are perceived and treated by others."[22] The term "ethno-religious" is sometimes used to capture the fact that ethnicity and religion can overlap and intertwine. People's ethno-religious identities don't have to do primarily with a system of religious beliefs that they may or may not embrace, or with various religious practices they may or may not take part in, but with who their parents and family are and how they are perceived, approached, and treated by others, regardless of their own wishes and preferences. They may regret and resist this, but there are limits to what they can do about it. The concept of ethno-religious identity is of increasing importance throughout the modern world. It is particularly significant where there are conflicts of interest between different nations, communities, and groups—for example, those to do with territory, recognition, esteem, and resources. Conflicts can be not only racialized but also what is sometimes termed "religionized," as people caught up in them seek to define and sharpen differences between "us" and "them," the self and the Other, and to rally support for themselves.

In setting out the ethnic dimensions of religious identity, CoRAB sought to navigate some extremely difficult terrain. On the one hand, religion (unlike gender, race, class, or sexual orientation) involves assent to a set of truth claims. In a free society, such truth claims must be contestable, particularly if they are to be allowed to affect public policy. It is surely legitimate, therefore, to hold that a particular religion or belief is damaging or irrational without being labeled a bigot. However, religions are not simply collections of propositions that can be weighed and contested. They are embodied in a common life that continues to evolve and change through interaction with the wider world. As I will show, the experience of community organizing provides many practical illustrations.

As we saw in chapter 1, there are three primary reasons for the hostility that Muslims face as an ethno-religious group. First, migration is wrongly blamed for the dilution of the "Christian character" of many secularizing democracies (in part because Christianity is falsely conflated with whiteness). Muslims bear the brunt of this false critique. Second, the intertwining of faith and politics in Islam is seen as problematic in societies where many Christians have been content to accept the false neutrality of liberal secularism with its attempt to exclude different communities' conceptions of the good from political debate. Third, since 2001, the experience of Islamist violence in Western democracies has been the catalyst for a surge in Islamophobic rhetoric and action.

In the sections following, I will explore the issue of integration policy and Islam by discussing two issues regarding which there are frequent concerns—Islamic attitudes toward women's leadership and violent Islamic extremism.

WOMEN'S LEADERSHIP

Many anti-Muslim polemicists focus on Islamic attitudes toward women, and the wearing of the hijab has become a totemic issue: A curious alliance between some liberal secularists and some on the Christian right see it as incompatible with Western culture. Whatever the intention, such attacks on the hijab have placed Muslim women on the front line of Islamophobic hate crimes. In the wake of the Brexit vote, many Muslim women in the Tower Hamlets neighborhood of East London (including colleagues working for Citizens UK) were cursed or spat at in the street as far-right extremists saw the decision to leave the EU as a vindication of their worldview.

As David Barclay has observed, Citizens UK comes under attack from liberals on both left and right for its willingness to work with mosques with "regressive" views on gender.[23] The reality is very different. Power within the Muslim community is more widely dispersed than its critics often acknowledge. Crucially, the process of engaging and developing leaders enables Muslim women to take a lead in the process of challenging structural injustices rather than being silenced in a debate dominated by white male critics.

Instead of lecturing Muslim women from afar on what they should and should not wear, responsible men, crafting a truly supportive response, would seek to build relationships by listening to Muslim women's experiences and interests. There is something deeply ironic about powerful white men attacking Muslims rhetorically (and sometimes physically) for their alleged silencing of women while showing no interest in the opinions or experience of those women.

In Tower Hamlets, motivations for wearing the hijab vary. Far from being a universal statement of submissiveness, enforced by men, there is a discernible trend to choose the hijab as a sign of Muslim pride and as a refusal to be subjugated by the rhetoric of Islamophobic men.

Our research in East London bears out the claim that ethno-religious cultures are not static. Constructive engagement with the wider society is changing the position of Muslim women in Tower Hamlets. The impact of community organizing on the internal life of institutions is bearing fruit, with women in East London Mosque and in Muslim women's groups such as Muslimaat developing as leaders through community organizing training and action alongside others. At St. George-in-the-East in Shadwell, these engagements have led to a request by local Muslim women for the church to partner with "Meals on Heels," a social enterprise they had founded to develop the confidence and economic independence of women in the area and to provide food to homeless people. (A similar process is exemplified by Lina Jamoul's story of the Mosque Foundation in Chicago.)

Our experience in East London is echoed in wider research across the country. In 2017 Citizens UK published *The Missing Muslims: Unlocking British Muslim Potential for the Benefit of All*, the report of its Commission on Islam, Participation and Public Life.[24] *The Missing Muslims* was the fruit of two years of listening to Muslims and their neighbors throughout the United Kingdom. Two themes surfaced: that "top-down" pressure to integrate is counterproductive and that Muslim women are in fact disadvantaged by the hostile rhetoric of people who claim to be concerned about their oppression.

Evidence of the first theme emerges repeatedly from the testimony given to the Citizens UK Commission:

The more we are told what it means to be British, the less British we feel. (Secondary School Student, West Midlands)

We dream and think in English, we know pop culture, yet I still do not belong. In Pakistan I am seen as British, but here I am questioned." (Adult Female Respondent, West Midlands)

You feel that you're British unless someone asks you to prove it. (Adult Male Respondent, London)

They [the media] convey a narrative where Muslims feel like second-class citizens. In the archives, my great grandfather has his war medals, but even someone like me who is patriotic is made to feel like a foreigner. (Adult Male Respondent, London)

The commission was itself an imaginative act of cross-community engagement. As Citizens UK Executive Director Neil Jameson explained,[25] Muslims involved in the alliance across the country were expressing increasing frustration about the way in which the national government and the national media misunderstood and misrepresented them. Since the instinctive response of organizing is to build relationships, Citizens UK gathered a group of commissioners from the world of government, the media, and commerce as well as the voluntary sector.[26] It asked them to engage in face-to-face dialogue with Muslims and their neighbors in Britain's most deprived and diverse communities.

Testimonies such as those cited above helped the commissioners to appreciate how counterproductive it is to stigmatize an entire community and its identity. As they observe in their report: "This increased scrutiny and coverage on 'Muslim' issues can result in an 'us vs. them' dichotomy, which produces its own cycle of separateness, with young Muslims growing up in a climate of being 'othered.' We have heard this view expressed particularly strongly by young people. For second generation Muslims, this lack of belonging can be exacerbated by not feeling fully accepted as British, but also by not being fully attached to their parents' cultural identity either."[27]

The second theme—the counterproductive effects of attacks on the hijab—was also reflected in the evidence presented to the Commission by the House of Commons Women and Equalities Select Committee 2016: "Muslim British women are 71% more likely than white Christian women to be unemployed, even when they have the same educational level and language skills. As well as suffering the [same] disadvantages of Muslim men relating to employment opportunities, some women also face pressures from their communities around education and employment choices, and particular issues of discrimination within the workplace around dress."[28] Further, "Muslim women can often face a compounded element of discrimination, owing to their religion, gender and ostensible markers such as the headscarf (hijab) and face-veil (niqab)—as well as a lack of support from within their own communities. Scarves and veils make Muslim women visibly recognisable, and thus faith identity becomes a very public one and is not easily disconnected from general misconceptions on Muslim identity."[29] This hostility undermines the central role Muslim women play in building relationships across communities. The Commission found that they play a vital role in "brokering relationships, whether it be at an interfaith level, at a social level (such as parent and toddler groups, coffee mornings, book clubs and the like) or with other community organizations."[30]

The process of congregational development, which churches in community organizing have harnessed to considerable effect, has huge potential to develop women's leadership within mosques. As the Commission notes in *The Missing Muslims*, "Some women told the Commission that the barriers to change in mosques are not the Imams, but the management committees who are often first-generation men, who are fiercely protective of a traditional culture. They note that when the younger generation are involved and able to play a part in leading, mosques and other institutions are often more open and more inclusive, and benefit from a wider range of professional skills to help solve problems."[31] This testimony reinforces Barclay's earlier critique of the "progressive tests" that people on both the left and right of politics have applied to Citizens UK's engagement with mosques. It is precisely as such engagement deepens that Muslim women are more likely to have their community leadership acknowledged and their power enhanced.

TACKLING VIOLENT EXTREMISM

For many right-wing critics, the main concern is not that mosques are socially conservative but that they are thought to be breeding grounds for extremism. Again, the evidence points in a different direction. In fact, increasing the resilience of mosques is key to tackling violent extremism.

The International Centre for the Study of Radicalisation and Political Violence published a detailed analysis titled *Recruitment and Mobilisation for the Islamist Militant Movement in Europe*. It concluded that, despite much media anxiety about "radical mosques," the radicalization process (insofar as it operates through mosques) largely consists in *detaching* people from their relationships with those institutions:

> Mosques play an integral part in the day-to-day lives of Muslim communities. They are not just centers for worship and spiritual enrichment, but they host educational activities, perform welfare functions and serve as a gathering place for different generations. . . . Given the centrality of the mosque in Muslim community life, it is logical that violent extremists have tried to exploit mosques as a place in which to find support and recruit followers. Simply put, there is no better and no more obvious place in which to meet large numbers of devout Muslims, who could be open to the religiously framed political message which Islamist militants hope to convey.[32]

According to this research, the institution of the mosque is very rarely the initiator of radicalization—but mosques are often infiltrated by those seeking to radicalize individual worshipers. Increasing awareness of this by imams and committees and increasing police surveillance mean that, while mosques are now places where radicals may come and "talent spot," their modus operandi is then to isolate their targets from the host institutions:

> This does not mean that mosques no longer play any role in the recruitment of violent extremists. . . . Members of Islamist militant groups still mix with worshippers, but—rather than stirring up trouble with the rest of the congregation—they will operate quietly, making themselves available to associates and befriending people whom they judge to be of interest. . . . Recruitment into Islamist militancy can occur wherever Muslims congregate, or where feelings of isolation and vulnerability can be exploited in order to socialize individuals into violent extremism. What seems to matter as much as—if not more than—particular locations are the individuals involved in the process.[33]

Isolating and stigmatizing institutions of the Muslim faith is therefore entirely counterproductive. Where mosques are better organized and have stronger internal relationships (particularly across ages—an issue that, as we saw, was raised in *The Missing Muslims*)—radicalization is less likely to happen. Where mosques are in deeper relationships with their neighbors, hostility and stereotyping are likely to diminish. This reinforces my earlier claim that trust and relationship are more contagious than extremism. The evidence presented to Citizens UK's commissioners also reinforces this analysis. The fear of extremism is in fact discouraging Muslim participation in public life: "There is recognizable concern about Islamist influence in public bodies and schools. However, the sentiment was expressed during hearings that every Muslim seeking to become involved in public life risks becoming branded an 'entryist.' This, in turn, dissuades Muslims from engaging in public life from the fear of 'raising their heads above the parapet.'"[34] As in the case of anxiety about "regressive" mosques, there is a danger that the anxiety about Islamic extremism will reinforce the conditions of isolation and persecution in which it is most likely to flourish. Dissuading Muslims from participating in wider civic life and weakening and isolating mosques simply backfires. A more helpful response would be to support mosques in developing stronger internal relationships and cultures that promote leadership from a wider spectrum of ages and in encouraging greater participation by Muslims in the lives of their neighborhoods.

The typical profile of a terrorist is not one of intense religious devotion. Terrorists tend to have fallen away from faithful Muslim practice into a world of petty crime, drug and alcohol use, and, frequently, domestic violence. Islamism offers a "redemptive narrative" that gives these lives meaning and the perpetrators an imagined status very different from the banality of their current lives. Once again we see the sharp contrast between Islamophobic stereotypes and realities. When community organizing helps mosques to listen to their young people, organize activities that reflect their interests, and help them discern common interests both with their elders and with the other institutions of their neighborhood, it both helps to strengthen the resilience of mosques and reduces the likelihood of radicalization and violent extremism.

The rhetoric and the policy prescriptions of right-wing populists intensify the very problem they claim to be addressing. In perpetuating the myth of a (rational, peaceable) West on an inevitable collision course with a (primitive, violent) Islamic world, they fail to recognize, or to care, that in fact *both* worlds perceive the other as violent. It is becoming increasingly clear that the violence of groups such as Da'esh is designed to provoke precisely this reaction from Western societies. The terrible irony is that the rhetoric of right-wing populists plays into the hands of the terrorists. One of the frequent refrains of the right wing is that those who criticize their approach have had their judgment distorted by "political correctness." They contend that the approach advocated here is dangerously naïve.[35] However, the reaction right-wing populists are advocating is the very one that Da'esh is seeking to provoke. And it is usually unwise to respond to terrorism with the very actions its perpetrators hope to elicit and then to exploit.

The violence of Da'esh is best understood not as an attack by some homogenous "Islam" on "the West." Da'esh is a radicalized sect that is currently at war with mainstream Islam. The casualty figures bear this out. The heaviest death toll from Islamic terror falls on Muslims, a fact that undermines the claim that the violence is somehow intrinsic to the faith itself. The purpose of the increasingly random and brutal attacks on Western countries—a truck driving through a crowd celebrating Bastille Day in Nice or a priest knifed while saying Mass in a Normandy village—is to goad the majority of Westerners into precisely the reactions being advocated by right-wing populists, namely, the scapegoating of Islam for these crimes.

This is borne out by the striking level of *mutual* fear recorded in the Pew Institute's research about attitudes in Islamic and Western countries. Whereas 50 percent of non-Muslim Westerners associate "Muslims" with violence, 66 percent of Muslims associate "people in Western countries" with this same quality.[36] To non-Muslims, the latter statistic may seem much more surprising than the former. However, it is only two decades since previously peaceful Christian neighbors systematically slaughtered the Muslims of Srebrenica on European soil. As my own organizing in East London has taught me, this is an experience that remains extremely salient to many Muslims, as do the military actions of the West in Iraq, Syria, Palestine, and other areas of the Middle East.

The research from the Pew Institute reveals the scale of the challenge of integration, but it also provides grounds for hope. If the challenge is *mutual* fear, the experience of community organizing—engaging with diverse communities around their existing experiences and interests and seeking to discern a common good—has obvious potential. What is required to integrate Muslims into British and American public life is a greater mutual understanding and empathy.

One small example from our research in Tower Hamlets may illustrate the point. There was a spate of "faith hate" incidents in which Bengali Muslim youths vandalized a local churchyard. In the aftermath of parallel incidents in local mosques (such as a pig's head being left outside one such place of worship), it would have been easy for this string of incidents to be narrated by each community in a way that reinforced the perception of the "Other" as hostile. Instead, Muslims and Christians came together to form the Stepney Fathers Group. They recognized a shared problem across the communities: a failure of engagement across the generations and a lack of activities and opportunities for young adults. The "Stepney Fathers" took action together to address it, and thus reduce the vandalism. It is in such modest acts of face-to-face encounter that strangers discover common interests, which replace suspicion and fear. In such settings they learn what it is to become active citizens together.

IMMIGRATION POLICY

This chapter has addressed the question of integration before addressing the question of immigration. The logic for this is simple: Until a nation is clear about its values, until its citizens decide to build a life together, there can be little clarity or consensus about how to welcome new citizens into that life and communicate the values it embodies.

By addressing the theoretical weaknesses generated by political liberalism it becomes possible to reframe the issue in terms of a negotiated pluralism. Issues of political process then become more evidently relevant, and community organizing can be appreciated as providing a way for new voices to engage. I now turn to the specific policy questions.

Luke Bretherton argues that many modern theorists either imagine borders as "filters" (in which everyone other than criminals should be let through) or "fences" (which seek to keep out the vast majority of migrants, allowing entry only to a well-qualified few).[37] Liberal political thought will oscillate between these two extremes, for it lacks any substantive understanding of the common good. The challenge for political liberals is neatly expressed in the argument of Alasdair MacIntyre: The modern nation-state is, for liberals, a paradoxical institution; that is, it presents itself as a "sacred institution" for which citizens should be willing to give up their lives while aiming at a kind of ethical neutrality, which means it has no substantive vision of the good by which to inspire its citizenry.

This unstable combination is exposed in debates about immigration. If nothing deeper binds its citizens together, it is very difficult for a liberal state to discern a basis on which to include or exclude others.

In one conception, then, immigration policy should allow *anyone* in, as citizens of a nation owe nothing more nor less to each other than they do to any other human being. As Bretherton observes, this is the position taken by many liberal theorists, most notably Michael Dummett and Peter and Renata Singer. However, the opposite argument could be made in terms of liberal democratic process. If (*pace* classical liberalism) the state is simply the guarantor of the rights and freedoms of its citizens, they have a right to decide who can and cannot come in, entirely on the basis of their economic interests.

Bretherton offers a third image, to place alongside filters and fences:

> We need to see borders as a *face* we present to the world. A face says that I am someone who deserves respect. I am not simply a piece of land to be bought and sold or a thing to make use of for a time. I have a personality and a way of doing things, but I am made for relationship and without coming into relationship with others who are different from me, I do not grow. . . .
>
> Borders are a means of framing and structuring this relationship and orienting a nation to the rest of the world in a way that presents an enquiring, confident, hospitable face rather than either a closed, insular hostile face turning away from relationship with the poor and vulnerable or a hopeless, insecure face that is used and lacks a sense of self-worth.

Like Rowan Williams's lecture on "British values," Bretherton's invocation of the face holds two truths together in creative tension. It acknowledges that, in a politics of negotiated pluralism, each nation's ethos will express a distinctive history and a distinctive way of negotiating the variety of conceptions of the good held by its diverse citizens. While each nation will have a different story and a different ethos, these are oriented toward some kind of *truthfulness*. As I argued in chapter 1, our diverse conceptions of the good are not simply rivals. They can be shared resources, helping us to deepen our understanding of what is genuinely good, beautiful, and true.

Liberal political theory has no account of the distinctive "face" each different nation might present toward the world. This is the void that MacIntyre exposes when he talks of the unstable combination of patriotic rhetoric and moral vacuity at the heart of the modern nation-state.

In Britain, as in the United States, the inability of liberalism to sustain such a conversation has led on to considerable anger and anxiety about immigration. An increasingly acrimonious debate has developed between progressive leftists (who, on the whole, favor a relaxed immigration policy) and the right-wing populists, who want to regard borders as fences (or, indeed, walls).

Not for the first time, the position of many on the progressive left turns out to disadvantage poorer communities. In their desire to be inclusive, supporters of open borders are aiding the process of commodification that has been so damaging to Britain's and America's poorest communities. The reduction by liberal economics of both land and labor to interchangeable units of production denies the distinctiveness of each human person and community. As Bretherton argues, "Thus the problem with seeing borders as filters and migration as simply a question of individual freedom of movement is that it fails to value the on-going integrity and worth of a particular *place* and [the fact] that migration does change places for better and for worse and that people are right to be concerned about the changes it will bring." In this 2012 essay, Bretherton went on to warn that "lack of attention to this concern and love of place" would "make plausible" racist rhetoric and exclusionary forms of nationalism.[38] Subsequent events have vindicated his warning call.

WHOSE VOICES?

It is not simply the immigration *policies* that have fueled right-wing populism. The problem has been compounded by the widespread sense that the *process* by which policy is formulated is one in which established working-class communities have little voice.

This tension has played out differently in Britain and the United States. In Britain, the recent increase in immigration has come from the Eastern European countries that joined the EU in 2004 and 2007, as well as from the Horn of Africa. Instead of making an honest case for such immigration or taking action to reduce it, successive British administrations have adopted a harsh rhetoric (to respond to voters' concerns) while presiding over significant net flows of immigration (because of its overall economic benefits). The net effect has been to stoke voters' anxieties while failing to address the substantive issues that concern them.

Across the Atlantic, the United States under President Obama saw tougher enforcement of existing laws. However, because of progressive opposition, the administration was reluctant to draw attention to the fact. As Andrew Sullivan observes, this served to stoke voters' anxieties and reduce the likelihood of a long-term settlement on the issue that could command widespread democratic support. He criticizes the progressive left for standing in the way of immigration reform: "The activist reaction—a rejection of most immigration enforcement or, with sanctuary cities, an open defiance of it—just makes this worse and renders a sane immigration compromise even more remote."[39] The approach taken by community organizing is to draw the voices of the most marginalized citizens into the political process. On first glance, it might seem as if immigration policy would be a "wedge issue" on which participants in organizing alliances must agree to disagree. Organizing proceeds on the basis of broad-based consensus, and it is hard to imagine its diverse institutions—representing members of the Congolese diaspora and white working-class residents in Barking—coming to a common view of the desirable level of immigration.

Citizens UK's Strangers into Citizens campaign emerged from the experience of both undocumented migrant workers and settled working-class communities. While the overall level of immigration was deemed a "wedge issue," the alliance was able to unite around the merits of a one-off amnesty for undocumented migrants.

The case for such an amnesty arose from the experience of both migrants and settled communities. Many of TELCO's churches and mosques had members trapped in the "twilight zone" of undocumented migration. This left them vulnerable to exploitation and unable to participate fully in society.

It also left them unable to contribute to the UK economy by paying taxes. While undocumented migrants accessed many public services, the funding for these services did not reflect their presence. In chapter 4 I mentioned the community organizing campaign around the quality of cleaning, catering, and care at Newham General Hospital. Alongside the effect of outsourcing the cleaning and catering staff, one of the key reasons for the low quality of care at Newham General was the gap between the total population of the borough and the official number of residents. The former number determined the demand for hospital services, while the latter (and much lower) number determined its funding. The gap was largely caused by undocumented migration.

For this reason, the Strangers into Citizens campaign spoke to the interests of both constituencies. In the process of campaigning alongside each other, long-standing residents came to know more of the life stories of undocumented migrants. They gained an increased appreciation of the forces that make people leave their homeland for an insecure existence in an alien and sometimes hostile setting.

The campaign ran from 2007 to 2010. While its main demand (for a one-off amnesty for undocumented migrants) was not granted, Citizens UK's work had a significant effect: "In terms of impact, the campaign did help push the government toward fast-tracking the 'legacy cases'—those that had been stuck in the Home Office system for many years—towards rapid and almost entirely positive decisions for an estimated 160,000 people."[40] The campaign for a one-off amnesty was combined with a call for a more effective immigration policy for the future. This was a significant departure from the default position of many left-liberals who are hostile to all attempts to enforce immigration controls. The Strangers into Citizens campaign did not take a position on how open or restricted the UK's borders should be. But it recognized that illegal immigration was undesirable for all sections of society. It left undocumented migrants in a "shadow land" with few rights and great vulnerability to unscrupulous landlords and employers. It also fueled the resentment of longer-standing communities, for it undermined the principle that the existing citizens of a nation should have democratic control over the admission of migrants. The solution proposed by Citizens UK—a pathway to citizenship for existing undocumented migrants, a realistic immigration policy and its robust enforcement—is needed on both sides of the Atlantic.

As in the case of integration, policy on immigration cannot be considered in isolation. Whatever level of immigration a nation decides to welcome, policies on wages and housing will be vital to ensure that migration does not intensify the commodification of labor and land. The campaign for community-owned housing described above exemplifies a vision of affordable housing that prevents *place* from disintegrating into mere *space*. In *Laudato Sí* Pope Francis highlights the importance of "human ecology" in urban planning: "In our rooms, our homes, our workplaces and neighborhoods, we use our environment as a way of expressing our identity. . . . We see how important it is that urban planning always take into consideration the views of those who will live in these areas."[41] The Nehemiah Housing won by East Brooklyn Congregations and the Community Land Trusts secured in East London exemplify this vision by creating space that local people have worked together to win and to design and by providing an economic model of home ownership and rental that promotes stable communities. Likewise, the campaign for a living wage has created a counterforce to the tendency for migration to erode the pay and conditions of existing workers.

In the United Kingdom, although the campaign has focused on persuading employers to pay a living wage, it has also had a demonstrable impact on government policy. In 2015 the Conservative government introduced a "national Living Wage" well below the level Citizens UK regards as necessary for workers but significantly above the previous minimum wage. The government decision was an ambiguous compliment to Citizens UK, and there was understandable concern within the alliance that the measure would make it easier for employers to resist pressure to pay the real Living Wage. It is a tribute to the strength of the organizing alliance that the number of companies that signed on to Citizens UK's Living Wage increased after 2015. This suggests that such campaigns can *both* secure a genuine Living Wage for an increasing number of workers *and*, by attracting attention to the issue of low pay, indirectly influence the statutory minimum wage in an upward direction. On each side of the Atlantic, a living wage is crucial to ensuring that immigration does not hurt the poorest of the citizens already resident in a country.

CONCLUSION

It is easy for policy-makers to be dismissive of questions of process, as if they are a distraction from addressing the most pressing economic and social issues. This chapter has shown why that dismissive attitude is mistaken. In addressing the process by which policy is formed, organizing ensures that the perspectives of the poorest and most marginalized communities are brought to bear on the issues at hand. All too often these perspectives are belittled and dismissed as regressive or bigoted in a discourse dominated by middle-class voices.

On the three issues I have considered—integration and "national values," the role of Islam in public life, and the shape of immigration policy—attending to the perspectives of the poor and marginalized is the key to discerning a positive way forward. Attention to the marginalized also sets these specific policy questions in a wider framework of economic justice. To treat immigration and integration in isolation from those wider issues is to ignore one of the key forces driving the rise in right-wing populism. When the voices of the poorest citizens are heard, it becomes obvious that any long-term solution will need to address what Pope Francis has called the "three Ls"—land, labor, and lodging.

CHAPTER 6

Engaging the Theoretical Debate II

Traditions, Pluralism, and Populism

In this chapter I want to engage more deeply with the theoretical debates on pluralism and populism to further illuminate the case for negotiated pluralism and inclusive populism. My focus will be on the importance of traditions and the mediating institutions that embody and transmit them, both of which are underestimated by contemporary liberal thinkers.

STOUT ON "TRADITIONALISM"

Alastair MacIntyre and Stanley Hauerwas are among the leading proponents of a new "traditionalism" in political theory and theology. It is a position that sharply contrasts with the political liberalism of John Rawls, which I discussed in chapter 3. In *Democracy and Tradition*, Jeffrey Stout describes himself as charting "an acceptable path" between these two positions as he develops a "pragmatic" account of the way differing *convictions* and traditions can coexist in a pluralist democracy.[1]

In this chapter, I will contest Stout's suggestion that such a pluralism involves some kind of *via media* between liberalism and traditionalism. I will argue that a healthy pluralism requires precisely the confidence in traditions—and of the mediating institutions that embody them—that MacIntyre and Hauerwas are seeking to recover.

Hauerwas's work focuses on the role of the Church as a community forming disciples and "embodying a social ethic." It draws heavily on MacIntyre's account of moral reasoning as something that can take place only in living traditions of inquiry and life. He argues that "The primary social task of the church is to be itself—that is, a people who have been formed by a story that provides them with the skills for negotiating the danger of this existence, trusting in God's promise of redemption." There is an echo in Hauerwas of the "Christian populism" we discussed at the end of chapter 3. Hauerwas writes that "Christian social ethics can only be done from the perspective of those who do not seek to control national or world history but who are content to live 'out of control.'"[2]

Stout criticizes MacIntyre and Hauerwas for their pessimism about the possibility of constructive engagement in a pluralist society. He argues that MacIntyre's own intellectual journey belies his stated pessimism—for contemporary society has provided the intellectual forums that have enabled MacIntyre to make a rational choice between a variety of "traditions of enquiry."[3]

In the case of Hauerwas, Stout embraces a number of his insights about the need to anchor ethical claims in communities of inquiry and practice but urges a "friendlier" and less polemical engagement between Hauerwas and the wider political culture, and also a greater focus on Christian engagement with non-Christians on issues of social justice.

Hauerwas is, in fact, deeply committed to the project of constructive engagement across different *convictions*. Indeed, he has characterized his theological project in the following terms: "What I've been trying to do all along is to *make the church worthy* of participating in the kind of political relationships sought by the Industrial Areas Foundation."[4]

So, far from being "unfriendly" to those outside the Church or arrogant about the Church's merits, Hauerwas's "ecclesial turn" aims to challenge and change the Church. He wants it to break free from an uncritical identification with the values of the dominant (liberal secular) culture or from being beguiled by coercive "top-down" power and instead to recover the sense that it is precisely by being *itself* that the Church becomes capable of being like salt, light, and yeast—and thus blessing the wider society. As I have argued, the practice of community organizing involves congregations' both deepening their roots in their distinctive habits and traditions (to counter the effects of commodification on their souls and relationships) and build relationships with institutions with different *convictions* (and, in particular, different conceptions of the good).

Neither Hauerwas nor MacIntyre is calling for Christians to isolate themselves or turn inward. Hauerwas's ecclesial turn seeks to refocus the Church on "being the Church" and embracing the reality of pluralism rather than seeking to control the wider polity. MacIntyre's own intellectual journey—and, indeed, the account he gives of rationality in *After Virtue* and *Whose Justice? Which Rationality?*[5]—is in fact a powerful argument for a pluralism of traditions. MacIntyre's contention is that ethical judgments need to be embedded in such traditions if they are to be rationally discussed and justified. The possibility of the kind of pluralist discourse that Stout advocates in *Democracy and Tradition* is, in fact, dependent on the existence of robust and distinct traditions.

VARIETIES OF "TRADITION"

There are, then, two distinct kinds of "tradition" at work in such negotiated pluralism. There are the traditions embodied in the mediating institutions of civil society, including its churches, mosques, and synagogues. They embody distinct *convictions* and make claims to truth that are, to some extent, mutually exclusive. As I argued in chapter 1, this does not render them incapable of dialogue. Indeed, there is a range of registers in which a constructive dialogue can occur (which I have termed "mutual witness," "negotiation," and "debate").

But, as I have argued in chapter 5 of this book, there is another kind of "tradition"—the story of how, in each particular democracy, citizens with different *convictions* have sought to build a common life and discern some common goods. Such a form of negotiation, as Stout rightly suggests, is necessarily "pragmatic." He writes: "I am trying to articulate a form of pluralism, one that citizens with strong religious commitments can accept and that welcomes their full participation in public life without fudging on its own premises."[6]

Such a pragmatism need not negate what is of value within liberalism: equality before the law, individual liberty, and the affirmation of fundamental human rights and responsibilities. Rather, it gives a fuller account of why different citizens have reason to accept these affirmations.

It needs to tell a genealogical story (of the kind attempted by Larry Siedentop) showing them to be rooted within the moral traditions on which this negotiation has drawn. Stout goes on to say: "I see this pluralism primarily as an existing feature of the political culture, not as a philosophical doctrine needing to be imposed on it. Our culture is already pluralistic in the relevant sense."[7]

Here I suggest that Stout is overly optimistic. He underestimates the extent to which political culture has been distorted by the damaging effects of a secularizing liberalism—effects that are rather more evident in 2019 than they perhaps were when he wrote *Democracy and Tradition* in 2004. Rather than seeking to steer an "acceptable path" between secularizing liberalism and the traditionalism of MacIntyre and Hauerwas, Stout needs to recognize that his vision of a pluralist public square can come about only when the traditions of civil society are renewed and respected. Stout's project and that of Hauerwas and MacIntyre are in fact interdependent. A Church that heeds their critique of liberalism will not turn its back on its neighbors but will be able to work with them more effectively for the common good.

POPULISM AND TRADITION: THE TEA PARTY

Just as an effective pluralism requires robust and vibrant traditions and institutions, so also does a healthy and inclusive populism. It is an inadequate appreciation of such traditions that underlies "fake populisms" of left and right alike. What is needed is a positive, tradition-based populism.

In *Prophets and Patriots*, Ruth Braunstein compares the populism of Interfaith (a faith-based community organizing alliance) with that of the Patriots (a grassroots group within the Tea Party movement in the United States).[8] She notes that both forms of populism had considerable debts to Saul Alinsky. The debt of Interfaith to Alinsky will already be obvious to readers of this book, but the debt of the Tea Party is probably more surprising. However, as Braunstein explains, the leaders and employees of FreedomWorks (the national organization that delivered training to local Tea Party movements) studied him closely and "were known to spread the 'Alinsky gospel,' in the words of one reporter, as they provided early support to emerging local Tea Party groups, including the Patriots."[9]

The work of Braunstein and of Laura Grattan helps us to identify some of key differences between the populism of the Tea Party and the inclusive populism of community organizing. In chapter 1 I explained that community organizing is financially independent, inclusive, and institution-based. Bauerstein's fieldwork demonstrates that Tea Party populism is both exclusive and individualistic, while Laura Grattan describes its financial dependence on vested interests.

Whereas community organizing exemplifies a populism that is inclusive and begins with those otherwise marginalized, Braunstein argues that the Tea Party's populism was exclusive and sought to reassert privilege: "The Patriots offered a story of American patriotism from the perspective of those who were once at its center, and sought a return to that position. Interfaith members offered an alternative version of that story, in which men and women at the social and political margins demanded inclusion and recognition as full members of the American people and active participants in the American project."[10]

As Braunstein explains, the Tea Party movement actively excluded both religious groups promoting social justice and all Muslims: "For the Patriots, there were common threads linking Muslims and religious groups promoting social justice—both sought to transform American society; and by undermining the individualized nature of God-given rights and the singularity of the Constitution, both threatened the very foundations on which American liberty rested."[11]

The exclusion of religious groups committed to social justice was a symptom of the Tea Party's deeply individualistic understanding of politics. While it was a movement within civil society, Braunstein shows that its understanding of politics was that the sole purpose of such collective action as a limitation of the activity of government. Whereas the community organizing of Interfaith "framed the citizenry as a set of overlapping and nested moral communities (e.g., their congregations, their neighborhoods, their city, or the nation as a whole) that have certain collective interests and moral obligations," the Patriots "framed 'the people' as a collection of autonomous individuals endowed with God-given rights to pursue their own self-interest."[12] For all the other ways in which the Patriots would vehemently reject Rawls's redistributive, interventionist vision of the state, they agree with him that the state should not promote a substantive conception of the good. Their conception of "freedom," like his, is voluntaristic.

As well as being exclusive and individualistic, the populism of the Tea Party lacked the financial independence of community organizing. This is a point made in Laura Grattan's study of the movement. The very groups that have benefited most from the economic impact of liberalism have funded and supported the Tea Party's version of populism. It is thus constrained by its embrace of liberal economics. The corporate interests that have funded the movement and spread its message have ensured that these boundaries are not transgressed. As Grattan notes, where "rebellious aspirations" did emerge—for example, when local Tea Party groups allied with environmentalists to block the corporate-state mergers responsible for the Keystone Pipeline—they were "easily circumscribed" by the powerful elite groups that provided the movement with money and publicity in the media.[13]

Braunstein and Grattan help us to see how each of the three divergences between the Tea Party and community organizing—its lack of financial independence, its failure to be inclusive, and its hostility to an active role for mediating institutions and the traditions they embody—has allowed this grassroots movement for small government to be the precursor to the authoritarian "fake populism" of President Trump. It is a cautionary tale and demonstrates why the "three I's" of community organizing (financial independence, inclusivity, and institutions) are all important if movements are to remain genuinely populist.

NINETEENTH-CENTURY AMERICAN POPULISM

Laura Grattan argues for an "aspirational democratic populism" that "cultivates people's rebellious aspirations not only to share in power, but to do so in pluralistic, egalitarian ways across established horizons."[14] Like Bretherton, she offers the nineteenth-century American populism of the People's Party as a example of this vision's being (at least partially) realized.

Grattan explains the central role played by the institutions of grassroots citizens:

The centralizing voice of the People's Party would have been disembodied and lifeless without its deep relations and looser affinities with myriad, decentered spaces of everyday Populist practice: the public work of cooperative farming; the insurgent rituals of boycotts and strikes; the political education carried out in rural lecture circuits, immigrant social halls, and union reading rooms; the revivalism of prohibition; the cross-cutting fabric of women's social networks; the disruptive energies of suffrage; and the resilient efforts of black communities to build schools, promote economic independence, and secure civil and political rights.[15]

As Grattan shows, the populist movement in the United States oscillated between an exclusivist position in which the frustrations of poorer white workers scapegoated African Americans and moments of interracial solidarity. At times the Populist Party used rhetoric that associated it with "a vicious strain of white working-class *ressentiment* that deepened as settlers encountered indigenous peoples and Mexicans at the United States' expanding frontiers and as Anglo-Saxon laborers clashed with immigrants and blacks in the nation's industrializing cities."[16]

However, popular movements were also developing within these communities. Some Populist organizers saw the potential here to develop political strategies that would "link the futures of black and white and farmer and laborer together."[17]

Grattan's account of nineteenth-century American populism helps us to understand the Tea Party (as a partly grassroots, partly elite–funded movement that draws on the nativist tropes of white *ressentiment*) and also to map out a path to a more constructive and inclusive populism rooted in the diverse institutions of white, black, and Hispanic working-class communities.

A POPULISM OF TRADITIONS?

Grattan criticizes the Occupy movement in the United States in a way that echoes my critique of its UK counterpart in chapter 1. As she observes, the American movement "failed to connect to the everyday politics of local communities. . . . Grassroots actors who had been addressing the same issues for decades—primarily in communities of color—were quick to question the representativeness of a largely white movement that suddenly gave face to their struggles."[18]

However, Grattan sees its predominantly white, middle-class nature as a flaw rather than an almost inevitable feature of the movement, given its wider set of attitudes. My argument in chapter 1 was that this exclusionary feature of Occupy flows from its embrace of a social liberalism, even as it vehemently rejects economic liberalism. Just as the Tea Party's populism is constrained by its embrace of economic liberalism and its dependence on powerful patrons who benefit from this liberalism, so (in a way Grattan does not fully recognize) is Occupy constrained by its embrace of social liberalism. In particular, it is constrained by its deployment of "progressive tests" that (as we saw in David Barclay's research) alienates it from more conservative working-class groups.

Grattan's overly generous reading of Occupy may flow from an omission from her wider account of "aspirational democratic populism." While her definition of populism emphasizes "rebelliousness" and "egalitarianism," it makes no reference to the substantive conceptions of the good that are essential—as I have argued in chapter 3—to resisting the ill effects of secularizing liberalism.

A credible critique of the *status quo* must draw on these substantive conceptions of goodness and justice rather than the bare assertion of the merits of "egalitarianism," "resistance to hegemony," or "rebellion." The building of broad-based coalitions for justice requires a radicalism that is genuinely respectful of tradition.

As Saul Alinsky recognized, a broad-based political movement that is genuinely rooted in the lives, values, and institutions of the poorest citizens will need to be both "revolutionary" and "conservative."[19] Sheridon Wolin's account of democracy casts an important light on the practice of community organizing, for it recognizes the role of (often "conservative") mediating institutions and the traditions they embody in resisting the overweening power of state and market. In Wolin's words, the aim of such grassroots democracy is "not to level in the name of equality or to cherish nostalgia but, by gaining some measure of control over the conditions and decisions intimately affecting the everyday lives of ordinary citizens, to relieve serious and remediable distress and to extend inclusion beyond the enjoyment of equal civil rights by making access to educational and cultural experiences and healthy living conditions a normal expectation."[20]

In the midst of the crisis of secular liberal politics, Wolin argues that such activity is a source of genuine energy and hope. What the polity and economy of liberalism render scarce for its citizens is "the direct experience of politics itself and the responsibilities of power." This is the "renewable resource" of grassroots populism—its source of strength even as it "runs against the grain of the most powerful institutions of society."[21] In this book I have retold some of these stories of energy and hope in the belief that the action of residents of some of our most deprived and diverse neighborhoods charts a course for the wider citizenry of both Britain and America.

CHAPTER 7

Inclusive Populism and the Renewal of Politics

After only two years in office (at the time of my writing), President Donald Trump has confirmed the fears of many Americans and friends of America around the world, that his rise to power is the product of deep defects in the political order. These defects are systemic. They are not caused by the weaknesses of any politician, nor can any such individual resolve them. This is one reason why Barack Obama could never have lived up to the rhetorical promise of his election. As we saw in chapter 4, the logic of his own words implied that the change most urgently needed could not be initiated from the White House. While politicians could certainly do more to respond to grassroots citizens' action, the hope and the responsibility for change do not ultimately lie with them. They lie with each of us.

It is no coincidence that Trump, the politician most closely identified with the phrase "fake news," is also the greatest beneficiary of "fake populism." In seeking to point out the intellectual contradictions in his pronouncements, liberals have treated Trump as an ordinary opponent. Neither Trump nor his supporters are interested in playing by the rules of the existing political game.

On both sides of the Atlantic, liberal opponents have sought to expose the contradictions of this "fake populism" rather than asking why the political order is displaying such morbid symptoms. While it is emotionally easy for liberals to demonize right-wing populists such as Trump, it is much harder for them to admit that the causes of his success lie very close to home.

The immediate causes of the rise in far-right populism are clear: an economic crisis whose pain has been distributed very unevenly (and fallen least on the institutions that generated it); increased flows of global migration (which often lacked the active consent of the receiving populations); and a campaign of Islamist terror (designed to provoke Western democracies into a counterproductive response). However, the pressure generated by these factors exposes a much longer-standing weakness in political liberalism. Even if the individual political careers of Trump, Farage, and Le Pen end in failure, these weaknesses are endemic and require urgent attention.

As Alasdair MacIntyre argued almost forty years ago, the central flaw of liberalism is its inability to recognize its own partiality. The citizens who adhere to liberalism are among the most privileged. Their unacknowledged intellectual partiality has social and economic consequences.

Writing when the dominance of political liberalism seemed rather more secure, Chantal Mouffe observed that its privileged supporters hid behind a rhetoric of historically inevitable progress—dismissing their opponents as backward and prejudiced: "The key word of this strategy is of course 'modernization' whose effect is to discriminate between those who are in tune with the new conditions of the modern, post-traditional world and those who still cling desperately to the past. To use 'modernization' in such a way is no doubt a powerful rhetorical gesture which allows them to draw a political frontier between the 'moderns' and 'the traditionalists or fundamentalists,' while at the same time denying the political character of their move.'"[1]

What liberals had conceived as the inevitable march of modernization was in fact a political choice. This choice benefited the most privileged while undermining the traditional institutions through which many of the less privileged articulated their values and interests. In the years since Mouffe's analysis was published, liberalism has lost its veneer of political inevitability. Its alienation of poorer communities has been a key factor in the rise of "fake populism."

As we saw in chapter 5, the poorest communities in American and British society—recent migrants and established working-class communities—share a surprising number of features. Both have suffered at the hands of laissez-faire economics. Both are exploited by rogue landlords, employers paying poverty wages, and payday lenders. And both value the supposedly divisive idea of tradition—whether the traditions of a specific religious community or those embodied in a substantive set of "national values."

Whereas liberalism regards these archaic and diverse traditions (and the institutions that perpetuate them) as divisive, they provide the poorest citizens with a vital bulwark against the forces that oppress them. These mediating institutions provide the building blocks for an authentic and inclusive populism. This is the only long-term antidote to the fake populisms of Trump, Farage, and Le Pen.

ORGANIZING, INEQUALITY, AND THE COMMON GOOD

The economic campaigns of IAF and Citizens UK can all be understood as forms of resistance to commodification.[2] As we have seen, both the institutions and the teachings of the Abrahamic faiths have been at the heart of this resistance. They have played a central role in the campaigns that have won a living wage for low-paid workers on both sides of the Atlantic, affordable community-led housing for tens of thousands of US citizens, and Britain's first anti-usury law in over a century.[3] While criticized for being divisive, religious institutions bring together the citizens who are physical neighbors across the boundaries of age, race, and social class.

Because religious congregations are so effective at sustaining grassroots relationships, they have come to be valued by many secular agents of community development. As David Barclay's research shows, secular agents often want the relational power ("social capital") of religious institutions without respecting the distinctive missions of such congregations. Engagement on such terms can only ever be skin deep. Community organizing is distinctive in its willingness to engage with religious congregations, just as it does with trade unions and schools, in a way that respects the distinctive ethos and purpose of each. It is only when secularizing liberalism gives way to a deep and respectful pluralism—engaging with the distinctive beliefs and spiritual practices of churches, mosques, and synagogues—that it can also harness their unique capacity for building and sustaining relationships. These relationships are vital in resisting the growth in economic and social inequality.

While political liberalism has held sway, there has been a quite staggering rise in inequality. Writing in 2010, Jeffrey Stout dramatized economic inequality using the image of a pyramid. It is, as he noted, a familiar metaphor: Most people would picture the distribution of wealth in our societies as a fairly standard pyramid, with a small number of rich people at the top and a large number of poorer people at the base. In reality, the shape of inequality is far more extreme. If we imagine a pyramid with a base little more than a foot wide and those earning $150,000 a little more than two feet above the base, the pyramid would be twenty stories high before it reached the executives who declared more than $10 million dollars in family income on their tax returns. As Stout observed, "It's more like a very shaky golf club that only a mythic giant could use, or, more accurately, a very long, very thin wire with a very heavy pyramid hanging on the end of it. That's what social stratification would actually come to if represented graphically in terms of yearly income. The figures would be staggering even if they referred to lifetime income. The dominant members of society are many stories up on the extremely narrow but very long wire."

As Stout went on to note, these economic inequalities generate, and are then further embedded by, inequalities in political power:

> The executives up at the top of our imaginary twenty-story [pyramid] not only have enormous incomes but are also running the megacorporations that in recent decades reshaped the world economy and then brought the whole thing to the verge of ruin. Top CEOs possess the power that comes from accumulating a vastly disproportionate amount of the economy's total wealth. They also possess the power that comes from administering the incentive and command structures of modern businesses, many of which are capable of achieving effects, for good or for ill, the world over.[4]

The hypocrisy of Donald Trump's rhetoric lies in his attempt to turn the citizens at the bottom of this pyramid against each other. The right-wing populism that he promotes is doubly "fake." It is not generated by ordinary citizens (and engages only at a superficial level with their institutions and the *convictions* they embody), and it does not address the root causes of their economic disenfranchisement. By contrast, the inclusive populism of IAF and Citizens UK draws together the diverse groups that are disadvantaged by our current economic order.

Neighbors do not discern a common good by stepping back from their distinctive moral and religious commitments. It is when they are more deeply rooted in their diverse and distinctive institutions that they find the inspiration and energy to act together for justice, and learn the habits that form them as democratic citizens. In each organizing alliance, the religious traditions offer vital resources for resisting the process of commodification, from the Jubilee laws of the Torah and the prohibitions against usury in the Qur'an to the teachings on economic justice in *Caritas in Veritate* and *Laudato Sí*.

It is no coincidence that a religious leader is the most prominent global opponent of both "fake populism" and the injustices of our current economic order. Pope Francis aims not to draw attention to himself (as yet another charismatic leader) but to encourage the development of the popular leadership that is essential to a healthy democratic culture. As Anna Rowlands explains: "Pope Francis makes a link between the micro processes of social love, small gestures that build the common good, and the macro processes of injustice. . . . Francis asks us to find ways to listen that will help make visible and vocal those who disappear within our urban culture: to overcome our own and our neighbors' anonymity. In urban communities driven by internal and external migrations, how do we create communities that enable us to become leaders with names and faces?"[5]

Democracy can flourish only when ordinary people become such leaders. As Francis told the Second World Meeting of Popular Movements, "The future of humanity is in great measure in your hands, through your ability to organize and carry out creative alternatives."[6]

FIVE CHALLENGES

This book has told the story of the creation of communities of active citizens. In these communities, institutions enable strangers to become fellow citizens—"leaders with names and faces." It has argued that politics must be re-imagined as an activity that places them at its heart and not at its periphery. In doing so, it offers a challenge, and an invitation, to some specific groups of people.

First, organizing invites the *progressive left* to move beyond its attachment to secularizing liberalism. On both sides of the Atlantic, supposedly populist movements such as Occupy have remained trapped within a self-defeating framework. Wedded to what Barclay calls "progressive tests," they have been unwilling to engage with those who disagree with them—a choice that explains why support for the progressive left remains disproportionately white and middle class.

Precisely because the progressive left excludes those it deems "exclusive" and "regressive," it remains a movement *for* rather than *of* the poorest communities. The danger of such advocacy is that the interests of activists do not align with those of the poorest citizens. The Occupy movement was a case in point: The activists chose what they thought of as principled failure rather than the negotiation and compromise involved in achieving genuine change.

The practice of organizing also offers an invitation to *Secular Humanists*. If Secular Humanism acknowledges that it is one tradition among many and abandons the pretense of being a neutral meeting-point for all traditions, it may be able to play an important role in the community organizing movement.

As I have argued elsewhere, the Secular Humanist movement in the United Kingdom is in a process of "schism" with regard to its embrace of genuine pluralism.[7] The National Secular Society remains wedded to the myth that a nonreligious public square could somehow be a neutral one. By contrast, the British Humanist Association is slowly embracing the logic of pluralism by arguing for Humanist chaplains alongside religious ones and for Humanist perspectives in religious education. Those of us who have a religious faith should embrace this warmly as a belated recognition that Secular Humanism is not a neutral default option but rather a definite and contestable belief system like any other.

In chapters 4 and 5 we explored in some detail the challenge organizing presents to *elected politicians*. Unlike the "fake populism" of the right, organizing has a genuine respect for the vocation to elected office. It does not regard the current political crisis simply as the fruit of individual corruption or deviousness, recognizing that politicians are no more nor less virtuous than the rest of humanity. What organizing challenges is the "top-down" conception of politics in which elected officials are expected to take all the initiative on economic and social issues. It requires politicians to become more responsive to, and respectful of, the initiatives of the mediating institutions of civil society. These institutions stand apart from party politics. However, they are still in a broader sense political in that they seek the good of the *polis* in ways that challenge the root causes of oppression and injustice as well as caring for those who suffer its ill effects.

This wider conception of politics is embodied in the ministry of Pope Francis, who has steered clear of engagement in partisanship but is still an unashamedly political figure. When Donald Trump accused him of being a "political man," Francis responded: "Thank God he said I am a politician because Aristotle defined the human person as an 'animal politicus.' So at least I am a human person. . . . As far as what you said about whether I would advise to vote or not to vote, I am not going to get involved in that."[8]

The example of Pope Francis brings us to the fourth of our challenges: the challenge community organizing presents to *those who lead our mediating institutions*. At a time when the institutions of civil society are under increasing pressure, organizing invites their leaders to believe that a process of developing grassroots leadership and sharing power can strengthen and renew their lives. Moreover, it shows that when institutions journey beyond their comfort zones and engage generously and confidently with their neighbors, they can be *more* faithful to their core mission. For religious institutions in particular, this last point is a crucial one. The experience of congregations involved in organizing is clear: Engaging across difference need not lead to a dilution in faithfulness.

There is a danger that, in their rejection of far-right populism, the leaders of our mediating institutions lapse into a discourse indistinguishable from that of liberalism—simply issuing "top-down" calls for greater tolerance and lamenting the divisive rhetoric of figures such as Trump and Farage. There needs to be a recovery of confidence in the vital roles of their own congregations, schools, and unions in reweaving trust, neighborhood by neighborhood, and a willingness to invest significant resources in the organizing process.

In particular, there is a great deal more that schools and trade unions can do to harness the capacity of community organizing for internal institutional development. The examples given in this book have been almost exclusively drawn from religious congregations—primarily because this was the focus of our empirical research, but also because these are among the institutions that have thus far done most to apply the lessons of organizing internally.

The final and most important challenge of community organizing is the one it poses to *every citizen*. The forces that are turning citizens into strangers may seem too strong to resist. The yawning inequalities of power and wealth, dramatized in Jeffrey Stout's image of the pyramid, can leave us passive and demotivated. "Ain't It Awful?" may be a depressing refrain, but in a curious way it can also be a falsely consoling one. It absolves us of power and therefore also of responsibility. Yet the story of community organizing shows that "people power" is not only needed; it is also possible. Indeed, the inclusive populism I have advocated is already beginning to emerge—in the United States, Britain, and a growing number of other countries.[9]

In the most deprived and diverse neighborhoods, power is being built by the residents who have the sharpest experiences of exclusion and injustice. Their stories map a path beyond both the failings of secularizing liberalism and the extremist forces threatening to overwhelm our common life. This path presents a challenge, and an invitation, to each one of us.

NOTES

PREFACE

1. Michael Gecan, *Effective Organising for Congregational Renewal* (Chicago: ACTA Publications, 2008), and Ruhana Ali, Lina Jamoul, and Yusufi Vali, eds., *A New Covenant of Virtue: Islam and Community Organising* (London: Citizens UK, 2012).

CHAPTER 1   A Populist Moment

1. Inaugural Address of President Donald J. Trump, 20 January 2017, https://www.whitehouse.gov/inaugural-address (accessed 1 July 2017).
2. "A Year after the First Women's March, Millions Are Still Actively Protesting Trump," Vox 1 July, 2018, https://www.vox.com/policy-and-politics /2018/1/23/16922884/womens-march-attendance (accessed 8 February 2018).
3. The cities are all located in the world's most powerful and wealthy nations: the United States (Chicago, Boston, San Francisco, Los Angeles, Houston, Dallas-Fort Worth, New York, and Washington, DC), China (Hong Kong), the United Kingdom (London), France (Paris), Russia (Moscow), Canada (Toronto), Saudi Arabia (Riyadh, Mecca, and Medina), Australia (Melbourne and Sydney), and the city-states of Singapore and Dubai.
4. "Faith on the Move—The Religious Affiliation of International Migrants," Pew Research Center, Religion & Public Life," 8 March 2012, http://www.pewforum.org/2012/03/08/religious-migration-exec/ (accessed 7 January 2015).
5. Harvey Cox, *The Secular City: Secularization and Urbanization (A Theological Perspective)* (New York: MacMillan, 1965).
6. Commission on Religion and Belief in British Public Life, *Living with Difference: The Report of the Commission on Religion and Belief in British Public Life* (Cambridge: Woolf Institute, 2015), 15.

7. "Pope Francis: 'The Danger Is That in Times of Crisis We Look for a Savior,'" *El Pais in English*, 22 January 2017, https://elpais.com/elpais/2017/01/21/inenglish/1485026427_223988.html (accessed 29 August 2017).

8. Luke Bretherton, *Resurrecting Democracy: Faith, Citizenship and the Politics of a Common Life* (New York: Cambridge University Press, 2015), 52.

9. This builds on Bretherton's contention, in chapter 1 of *Resurrecting Democracy*, that community organizing is a form of "political populism."

10. The methodology and scope of this research is described in the preface.

11. Jeffrey G. Williamson, "Global Migration," *Finance and Development* 43: 3 (September 2006), http://www.imf.org/external/pubs/ft/fandd/2006/09/williams.htm (accessed 9 February 2018).

12. Ibid.

13. See, for example, chapter 1 of John Rawls, *Political Liberalism* (New York: Columbia University Press, 1993).

14. See Commission on Religion and Belief, *Living with Difference*, chapter 2, and the annual British Social Attitudes Surveys, which chart the decline in religious practice and affiliation in more detail. See also Tim Thorlby, *Love, Sweat and Tears: Church Planting in East London* (London: Centre for Theology and Community, 2015), and Beth Green, Angus Ritchie and Tim Thorlby, *Church Growth in East London: A Grassroots View* (London: Centre for Theology and Community, 2016).

15. See, for example, Toby Young, "If You Don't Like Britain Being Christian . . . Leave," in *The Sun*, 8 December 2015, https://www.thesun.co.uk/archives/news/833959/toby-young-if-you-dont-like-britain-being-christian-leave/ (accessed 14 July 2016).

16. Commission on Religion and Belief, *Living with Difference*, 15.

17. Pew Research Center, "America's Changing Religious Landscape," 12 May 2015, http://www.pewforum.org/2015/05/12/americas-changing-religious-landscape/ (accessed 13 February 2018).

18. "Tony Blair Pushes Back against "Frightening Authoritarian Populism," *Guardian*, 17 March 2017, https://www.theguardian.com/politics/2017/mar/17/tony-blair-launches-pushback-against-frightening-populism (accessed 30 May 2017).

19. See John Rawls, *A Theory of Justice* (Oxford: Oxford University Press, 1971), *The Law of Peoples* (Cambridge, MA: Harvard University Press, 1999), and especially his *Political Liberalism* and Robert Nozick's *Anarchy, State and Utopia* (New York: Basic Books, 1974).

20. It is worth noting that such peace is to be guaranteed only *within* the nation-state, to which citizens' other loyalties are expected to be subservient. As William Cavanaugh has observed, the nation-state demands such

a loyalty from members of different religions that they be willing to kill fellow believers from other nation-states. Violence has not been removed from the body politic; rather, the basis for citizens' killing has been changed. See William Cavanaugh, *Theopolitical Imagination: Discovering the Liturgy as a Political Act in an Age of Global Consumerism* (Edinburgh: T&T Clark, 2002), 32f.

21. Chantal Mouffe, *On the Political: Thinking in Action* (London: Routledge, 2005), 20–21. Luke Bretherton discusses some of the differences between Mouffe's vision of politics and the conception of politics expressed in community organizing in chapter 6 of his *Resurrecting Democracy: Faith, Citizenship and the Politics of a Common Life* (New York: Cambridge University Press, 2015).

22. Alasdair MacIntyre, "A Partial Response to My Critics," in John Horton and Susan Mendus, eds., *After MacIntyre: Critical Perspectives on the Work of Alasdair MacIntyre* (Notre Dame, IN: University of Notre Dame Press, 1994), 303.

23. See Luke Bretherton, *Christianity and Contemporary Politics: The Conditions and Possibilities of Faithful Witness* (Oxford: Wiley-Blackwell, 2010), 37–45, on the ways in which government-sponsored initiatives designed to generate "social cohesion" between "faith communities" have in fact generated more intercommunal competition and tension.

24. I have capitalized "Secular Humanist," along with "Secular Humanism," to reflect my argument that Secular Humanism should not be viewed as neutral but as a substantive position of its own alongside Christianity, Islam, Judaism, and other *religions et convictions.*

25. Laura Grattan, *Populism's Power: Radical Grassroots Democracy in America* (New York: Oxford University Press, 2016), 159.

26. Thomas B. Edsall, "The Democratic Party Is in Worse Shape than You Thought," *New York Times*, 8 June 2017, and YouGov UK, "How Britain Voted at the 2017 General Election, https://yougov.co.uk/news/2017/06/13 /how-britain-voted-2017-general-election/ (accessed 13 February 2018).

27. David Barclay, *Making Multiculturalism Work: Building Relationships across Deep Difference* (London: Theos, 2013).

28. Ibid., 28.

29. Larry Elliott, "With Politics Turned on Its Head, Labour Sticks to Brexit Ambiguity," *Guardian*, 24 June 2017, https://www.theguardian.com /politics/2017/jun/25/with-politics-turned-on-its-head-labour-sticks-to -brexit-ambiguity (accessed 30 June 2017).

30. "Election 2017: How the UK Votes in 7 Charts," *Financial Times*, 9 June 2017.

31. Pope Francis, *Evangelii Gaudium: Apostolic Exhortation on the Proclamation of the Gospel in Today's World*, 24 November 2013, http://w2

.vatican.va/content/francesco/en/apost_exhortations/documents/papa
-francesco_esortazione-ap_20131124_evangelii-gaudium.html (accessed 1
July 2017), 232.

32. Pope Francis, Speech to the Second World Meeting of Popular
Movements, Santa Cruz de la Sierra, 9 July 2015, http://w2.vatican.va/content
/francesco/en/speeches/2015/july/documents/papa-francesco_20150709
_bolivia-movimenti-popolari.html (accessed 30 June 2017).

33. In conversation with the author, 18 December 2018.

34. Social Integration Commission, *Kingdom United: Thirteen Steps to
Tackle Social Segregation* (London: Social Integration Commission, 2014), 2.

35. Ibid., 9.

36. International Centre for the Study of Radicalisation and Political
Violence, *Recruitment and Mobilisation for the Islamist Militant Movement in
Europe* (London: International Centre for the Study of Radicalisation and Po-
litical Violence, 2007), 19.

37. Harry Boyte, *Everyday Politics: Reconnecting Citizens and Public Life*
(Philadelphia: University of Pennsylvania Press, 2004), 58.

38. Saul Alinsky, *Rules for Radicals: A Pragmatic Primer for Realistic
Radicals* (New York: Random House, 1971), 53f.

39. Chantal Mouffe, *Agonistics: Thinking the World Politically* (London:
Verso, 2013), 3.

CHAPTER 2   Community Organizing as Inclusive Populism

1. Baroness Sayeeda Warsi, Britain's first Muslim cabinet minister,
tweeted asking, "If Sadiq Khan isn't an acceptable enough Muslim to stand for
London mayor, which Muslim is?" See also this blog entry by the chairman
of the Conservative Muslim Forum: "Mohammed Amin: I'm a Conservative, and voted for Zac. But I was disgusted by his repeated, risible attempts to
smear Khan," *Conservativehome*, 7 May 2016, http://www.conservativehome
.com/platform/2016/05/mohammed-amin-im-a-conservative-and-voted-for
-zac-but-i-was-disgusted-by-his-repeated-risible-attempts-to-smear-khan
.html (accessed 13 July 2016).

2. "Ken Livingstone Suspended from Labour after Hitler Remarks,"
Guardian, 28 April 2016, http://www.theguardian.com/politics/2016/apr/28
/ken-livingstone-suspended-from-labour-after-hitler-remarks (accessed 13
July 2016).

3. Alinsky was the pioneer of community organizing and the founder
of the Industrial Areas Foundation (IAF), which is the primary community

organizing movement in the United States and Canada. Neil Jameson, founder of Citizens UK, was first trained in organizing in the United States, and there continues to be a formal partnership between the two movements.

4. Jay MacLeod, *Community Organising: A Practical and Theological Evaluation* (London: Christian Action, 1993), 1.

5. Tim Conder and Dan Rhodes, *Organizing Church: Grassroots Practices for Embodying Change in Your Congregation, Your Community, and Our World* (St. Louis: Chalice Press, 2017), 29.

6. The story is told in more detail in Frank Pierson, "What Happened in Vegas: Battling Nevada's Underage Sex Trade," *Commonweal Magazine*, 9 September 2015, https://www.commonwealmagazine.org/what-happened -vegas (accessed 18 October 2017).

7. Conder and Rhodes, *Organizing Church*, 29.

8. Alinsky, *Rules for Radicals*, 162.

9. "Signature Accomplishments," *Industrial Areas Foundation*, 2018, http://www.industrialareasfoundation.org/content/signature-accomplishments (accessed 17 October 2018).

10. Jeffrey Stout, *Blessed Are the Organized: Grassroots Democracy in America* (Princeton, NJ: Princeton University Press, 2010), 92.

11. Gecan, *Effective Organising for Congregational Renewal*, 8.

12. Sarfraz Jeraj, "Taking Public Action on Mixed Gender Hospital Wards," in Ruhana Ali, Lina Jamoul, and Yusufi Vali, eds., *A New Covenant of Virtue: Islam and Community Organising* (London: Citizens UK, 2012), 28.

13. Dilowar Khan, "A Community Centre for All," in Ruhana Ali et al., *A New Covenant of Virtue*, 39–41.

14. Matthew Bolton, *How To Resist: Turn Protest to Power* (London: Bloomsbury, 2017), 72.

15. In conversation with the author, 18 December 2018.

16. "Living Wage," *Citizensuk*, www.citizensuk.org/living wage (accessed 8 February 2018).

17. "Signature Accomplishments," *Industrial Areas Foundation*, http:// www.industrialareasfoundation.org/content/signature-accomplishments (accessed 17 October 2017).

18. Stout, *Blessed Are the Organized*, 192–93.

19. From Matt McDermott, "A Jewish Organizing Story," in Gecan, *Effective Organizing for Congregational Renewal*, 44–48.

20. This is the first of a series of quotes from interviews that were part of our research.

21. This is the final quote from our research in this chapter.

22. Church Urban Fund, *Faithful Representation: Faith Representatives on Local Public Partnerships* (London: Church Urban Fund, 2006), and Rachael Chapman, "Faith and the Voluntary Sector: Distinctive Yet Similar?," in Adam Dinham, Robert Furbey, and Vivien Lowndes, eds., *Faith in the Public Realm: Controversies, Policies and Practices* (London: Policy Press, 2009), 212, cited in David Barclay, *Making Multiculturalism Work: Building Relationships across Deep Difference* (London: Theos, 2013), 35–36.

23. Adam Dinham et al., *Faith in the Public Realm*, 11, cited in Barclay, *Making Multiculturalism Work*, 36.

24. Barclay, *Making Multiculturalism Work*, 40.

25. See, for example, Robert Putnam, *Bowling Alone: The Collapse and Revival of American Community* (New York: Simon and Schuster, 2000); Richard Sennett, *The Corrosion of Character: The Personal Consequences of Work in the New Capitalism* (New York: W. W. Norton, 1998).

26. Stout, *Blessed are the Organized*, 38–39.

27. Conder and Rhodes, *Organizing Church*, 72–73.

28. See http://www.interfaithfunders.org/CongregationOrganizing.

29. *Organized Communities, Stronger Schools: Impact of Community and Youth Organizing on Public School Reform* (Providence, RI: Annenberg Institute for School Reform, Brown University, May 2009).

30. From Lina Jamoul, "A Muslim Organizing Story," in Gecan, *Effective Organising*, 35–39.

31. In conversation with the author.

CHAPTER 3   Engaging the Theoretical Debate I

1. John Rawls, *Political Liberalism* (New York: Columbia University Press, 1993), 15.

2. Rawls introduces the "veil of ignorance" in *A Theory of Justice* (Oxford: Oxford University Press, 1971) but has modified his account in response to critics,—so I will be engaging with the versions of the thought experiment that are laid out in his *Political Liberalism* and *The Law of Peoples* (Cambridge, MA: Harvard University Press, 1999).

3. Rawls, *Political Liberalism*, 16.

4. By "moral constructivism" I mean the view that there are answers to moral questions *because* there are correct procedures for arriving at them, in contrast to the morally realist assertion that there are moral truths or facts that exist independently of those procedures and that those procedures enable humans to comprehend.

5. I offer a brief taxonomy in the first chapter of my *From Morality to Metaphysics: The Theistic Implications of our Ethical Commitments* (Oxford: Oxford University Press, 2012).

6. This is a point I develop at greater length in my discussion of Christine Korsgaard (who is, like Rawls, a moral constructivist) in *From Morality to Metaphysics*, 90ff.

7. Chantal Mouffe, *Agonistics: Thinking the World Politically* (London: Verso, 2013), 8–9.

8. Larry Siedentop, *Inventing the Individual: The Origins of Western Liberalism* (London: Allen Lane, 2014).

9. Ibid., 29.

10. See, for example, 1 Corinthians 1:26–30.

11. John Milbank and Adrian Pabst, *The Politics of Virtue: Post-Liberalism and the Human Future* (London: Rowman and Littlefield, 2016), 33.

12. Warren Quinn, "Putting Rationality in Its Place," in Rosalind Hursthouse, Gavin Lawrence, and Warren Quinn, eds., *Virtues and Reasons: Philippa Foot and Moral Theory* (Oxford: Clarendon Press, 1996), 190. I discuss this in more detail in *From Morality to Metaphysics*, 102ff. Quinn's position is diametrically opposed to Rawls's view, articulated in part 3 of *A Theory of Justice*, that we can understand the goodness of something in terms of its being rational to want it.

13. Milbank and Pabst, *Politics of Virtue*, 258–59.

14. Patrick Deneen, *Why Liberalism Failed* (New Haven, CT: Yale University Press, 2018), 31, 37.

15. Ibid., 61.

16. Alexis de Tocqueville, quoted in Sheldon Wolin, *Tocqueville between Two Worlds: The Making of a Political and Theoretical Life* (Princeton, NJ: Princeton University Press, 2001), 210.

17. Ibid., 190.

18. Toqueville, quoted in ibid., 191.

19. Peter Brown, *Power and Persuasion in Late Antiquity: Towards a Christian Empire* (Madison: University of Wisconsin Press, 1992), 74.

20. Ernesto Cortés, "Towards A Democratic Culture," *Kettering Review*, Spring 2006, 48.

CHAPTER 4   Community Organizing: Six Challenges

1. Ann Coulter, "Obama: Lucifer Is My Homeboy," 17 September 2008, http://www.anncoulter.com/columns/2008-09-17.html (accessed 17 October 2017).

2. Luke Bretherton, *Resurrecting Democracy: Faith, Citizenship and the Politics of a Common Life* (New York: Cambridge University Press, 2015), 52.

3. Ibid., 53.

4. Quoted in David Barclay, *Making Multiculturalism Work: Building Relationships across Deep Difference* (London: Theos, 2013), 28.

5. Ibid., 28–29.

6. Ibid., 29.

7. Ibid., 30.

8. Mark Lilla, *The Once and Future Liberal: After Identity Politics* (New York: HarperCollins, 2017), 117–18.

9. Lilla, *Once and Future Liberal*, 118–19. Andy Walton, in *Is There a Religious Right in Britain?* (London: Theos, 2013), offers an interesting analysis of why the issue has not played the same role in UK politics.

10. Saul Alinsky, *Reveille for Radicals* (New York: Vintage Books, 1969), xvi.

11. Jacques Maritain, letter of 15 May 1962 to Alinsky, in Bernard Doering, ed., *The Philosopher and the Provocateur: The Correspondence of Jacques Maritain and Saul Alinsky* (Notre Dame, IN: University of Notre Dame Press, 1994), 89, quoted in Luke Bretherton, *Christianity and Contemporary Politics: The Conditions and Possibilities of Faithful Witness* (Oxford: Wiley-Blackwell, 2010), 93 (emphasis in original).

12. Jay MacLeod, *Community Organising: A Practical and Theological Evaluation* (London: Christian Action, 1993), 4.

13. Mary Beth Rogers, *Cold Anger: A Story of Faith and Power Politics* (Denton: University of North Texas Press, 1990), 94-5.

14. Andrea B. Coulson and James Bonner, *Living Wage Employers: Evidence of UK Business Cases* (Glasgow: University of Strathclyde, 2015), https://www.livingwage.org.uk/news/new-evidence-business-case-adopting-living-wage (accessed 11 February 2018).

15. Chris Shanahan, *A Theology of Community Organising: Power to the People* (London: Routledge, 2013), 120.

16. Ibid., 144–45.

17. "Full Text of Obama's Candidacy Speech," *Denver Post*, 10 February 2007, https://www.denverpost.com/2007/02/10/full-text-of-obamas-candidacy-speech/ (accessed 20 December 2018).

18. Examples include Trump's unwillingness to unequivocally disown the violent neo-Nazi protests in Charlottesville in August 2017 (see *Trump Defends Initial Remarks on Charlottesville; Again Blames "Both Sides"* in *New York Times*, 15 August 2017, and his derogatory remarks about immigrants coming to the United States from "shithole countries" in January 2018 (see

https://edition.cnn.com/2018/01/11/politics/immigrants-shithole-countries
-trump/index.html, accessed 15 February 2018).

19. Ta-Nehisi Coates, "The First White President," in *The Atlantic*, October 2017, https://www.theatlantic.com/magazine/archive/2017/10
/the-first-white-president-ta-nehisi-coates/537909 (accessed 28 September
2017).

20. "US Election Results: The Maps and Analysis That Explain Donald
Trump's Shock Victory to Become President," *Telegraph*, 15 October 2016,
http://www.telegraph.co.uk/news/0/us-election-results-and-state-by-state
-maps/ (accessed 15 February 2018).

21. Jeffrey Stout, *Blessed Are the Organized: Grassroots Democracy in
America* (Princeton, NJ: Princeton University Press, 2010), 275.

22. Ibid., 271–74.

23. Barack Obama, *Dreams from My Father: A Story of Race and Inheritance* (New York: Three Rivers Press, 2004), 276, cited in Stout, *Blessed Are the
Organized*, 263.

24. Quoted in Stout, *Blessed Are the Organized*, 260.

25. Ibid., 276.

26. Madeline Bunting, "How Cameron Fell Out of Love with His Citizen Organisers," *Guardian*, 14 February 2011.

27. Pope Francis, *Evangelii Gaudium: Apostolic Exhortation on the Proclamation of the Gospel in Today's World* (2013), http://w2.vatican.va/content
/francesco/en/apost_exhortations/documents/papa-francesco_esortazione-ap
_20131124_evangelii-gaudium.html (accessed 1 July 2017), 223.

28. Stout, *Blessed Are the Organized*, 8–9.

29. Mike Gecan, *Going Public: An Organizer's Guide to Citizen Action*
(Boston: Beacon Press, 2002), 136f., and Stout, *Blessed Are the Organized*,
128.

30. Barclay, *Making Multiculturalism Work*, 40–41.

31. Cf. Karl Polanyi, *The Great Transformation* (Boston: First Beacon,
1957), 73f.

32. Jonathan Freedman, "Heard the One about a Rabbi, an Imam and a
Priest Who Walk into a Bank?," *Guardian*, 22 July 2009.

33. Pope Benedict XVI, *Caritas in Veritate*, 29 June 2009, http://w2
.vatican.va/content/benedict-xvi/en/encyclicals/documents/hf_ben-xvi_enc
_20090629_caritas-in-veritate.html (accessed 14 August 2018), 34.

34. Contribution to Italian Ecumenical Day of Christian-Islamic Dialogue, October 2009, cited in Angus Ritchie and David Barclay, eds., *God and
the Moneylenders: Faith and the Battle against Exploitative Lending* (London:
Contextual Theology Centre, 2013).

35. David Barclay records some of the stories that emerged from London Citizens' listening campaigns in "Payday Lending and the Experience of Borrowers," in Barclay and Ritchie, *God and the Moneylenders*, 9–20.

36. Luke Bretherton, "Neither a Borrower nor a Lender Be?," in Angus Ritchie, ed., *Crunch Time: A Call to Action* (London: Contextual Theology Centre, 2010), 22.

37. Ibid., 30.

38. Vincent D. Rougeau, "Rediscovering Usury: A Reprise of an Argument from 1996 for Interest Rate Controls on Credit Cards," in ibid., 46.

39. Our research has focused on the Abrahamic faiths, which have played the greatest role in community organizing on both sides of the Atlantic. It is important to note, before moving on from this discussion, the slight but growing participation in organizing by institutions of the Dharmic faiths—and the importance of further research on this dimension of the movement's pluralism.

40. Sarah Bachelard, "The Ego-Driven Church: On the Perils of Christian Activism," ABC Religion and Ethics blog, 19 December 2017, http://www.abc.net.au/religion/articles/2017/12/19/4782549.htm (accessed 1 January 2018).

41. Centre for Theology and Community and Citizens UK, Congregational Development Action Learning Community Handbook (unpublished, 2014), 13.

42. Austen Ivereigh, *The Great Reformer: Francis and the Making of a Radical Pope* (London: Allen and Unwin, 2014), 303.

43. P. Rodari, "Conversaciones con Víctor Manuel Fernández," *Iglesia Viva* 259 (July–September 2014): 65, quoted in Rafael Luciani, *Pope Francis and the Theology of the People* (New York: Orbis Books, 2017), 9.

44. Luciani, *Pope Francis and the Theology of the People*, 9.

45. The story of the renewal of St. George-in-the-East is told in chapter 8 of Tim Thorlby, *A Time to Sow: Anglican Catholic Church Growth in London* (London: Centre for Theology and Community, 2017).

46. Martin Robbins, "Why Are Women More Opposed to Abortion?," Guardian, 30 April 2014 , https://www.theguardian.com/science/the-lay-scientist/2014/apr/30/why-are-women-more-opposed-to-abortion (accessed 8 January 2018).

47. The inadequate representation of women in the Church was raised by Pope Francis months after his election, when he commented on that, saying, "It is necessary to broaden the opportunities for a stronger presence of women in the church" (reported in the *National Catholic Reporter*, 25 September 2013).

48. "Nearly Six-in-Ten Americans Say Abortion Should Be Legal in All or Most Cases," *Factank*, Pew Research Center, 17 October 2018, www

.pewresearch.org/fact-tank/2017/07/07/on-abortion-persistent-divides
-between-and-within-the-two-parties-2/ (accessed 8 February 2018).

CHAPTER 5   Integration, Islam, and Immigration

1. Michael Gove, quoted in *Prospect*, October 2007, http://www
.prospectmagazine.co.uk/magazine/insearchofbritishvalues1#.U5bYjpRdWIk
(accessed 11 October 2017).

2. Shamit Saggar and Will Somerville, *Building a British Model of Integration in an Era of Immigration: Policy Lessons for Government* (Washington,
DC: Migration Policy Institute, 2012), 10–11.

3. Rowan Williams, "Multiculturalism: Friend or Foe?," lecture given
at Toynbee Hall, East London, 16 May 2007, http://rowanwilliams.arch
bishopofcanterbury.org/articles.php/1152/multiculturism-friend-or-foe
-archbishops-lecture (accessed 11 October 2017).

4. Commission on Religion and Belief in British Public Life (CoRAB),
*Living with Difference: The Report of the Commission on Religion and Belief in
British Public Life* (Cambridge: Woolf Institute, 2015), 66.

5. Justin Welby, quoted in *Daily Telegraph*, 8 November 2016.

6. *Catholic Herald*, 17 July 2017.

7. Caitlin Burbridge, *Faith and the Politics of "Other": Community Organizing amongst London's Congolese Diaspora* (London: Contextual Theology
Centre, 2013), 22–23.

8. Ibid., 24–28.

9. Ibid., 24–25.

10. Ibid., 28.

11. Ibid., 17.

12. Angus Ritchie, quoted in Scott Stephens, ed., "After Brexit: The
Referendum and Its Discontents," *ABC Religion & Ethics blog*, http://www
.abc.net.au/religion/articles/2016/06/24/4488874.htm (accessed 24 October
2017).

13. Two TELCO leaders from the Salvation Army, Captains Nick Coke
and John Clifton, blogged on their differing attitudes toward Brexit and the
value of community organizing in charting a common way forward in "Five
Ways to Live Post-Brexit," http://matchfactory.org/2016/06/five-ways-to-live
-post-brexit/ (accessed 18 October 2017).

14. Firth and Chowdhury had previously worked for Citizens UK, and
Chowdhury has since been a colleague at CTC. This research is being con-
ducted through a new, independent campaigning organization called We
Can Win.

15. Sotez Chowdhury, correspondence with the author, 17 October 2017.

16. D. Eversley, and F. Sukdeo, *The Dependants of the Coloured Commonwealth Population of England and Wales* (London: Institute of Race Relations, 1969), cited in David Owen, *Ethnic Minorities in Great Britain: Patterns of Population Change, 1981–91* (Warwick, UK: University of Warwick Centre for Research in Ethnic Relations, 1995), 1.

17. Mark Lilla, *The Once and Future Liberal: After Identity Politics.* New York: HarperCollins, 2017, 61.

18. Ibid., 109–10.

19. Ibid., 76–77.

20. Jeffrey Stout, *Blessed Are the Organized: Grassroots Democracy in America* (Princeton, NJ: Princeton University Press, 2010), 39.

21. Tomás Jiménez, *Immigrants in the United States: How Well Are They Integrating into Society?* (Washington, DC: Migration Policy Institute, 2011), 18–19.

22. CoRAB, *Living with Difference*, 14.

23. David Barclay, *Making Multiculturalism Work: Building Relationships across Deep Difference* (London: Theos, 2013), 28–29.

24. Citizens Commission on Islam, Participation & Public Life, *The Missing Muslims: Unlocking British Muslim Potential for the Benefit of All* (London: Citizens UK, 2017).

25. Neil Jameson, in conversation with the author.

26. The commission was chaired by Conservative MP and former attorney general Dominic Grieve and included *Daily Mail* and *Telegraph* columnist Peter Oborne, Sir Trevor Chinn from the Jewish Leadership Council, and Jenny Watson, former chair of the Electoral Commission.

27. Citizens Commission, *The Missing Muslims*, 23.

28. House of Commons Women and Equalities Select Committee 2016, cited in Citizens Commission, *The Missing Muslims*, 33.

29. Ibid., 33.

30. Citizens Commission, *The Missing Muslims*, 25.

31. Ibid., 42.

32. International Centre for the Study of Radicalisation and Political Violence, *Recruitment and Mobilisation for the Islamist Militant Movement in Europe* (London, 2007), 19.

33. Ibid., 22 and 27.

34. Citizens Commission, *The Missing Muslims*, 45.

35. See, for example, Sam Harris, "Head-in-the-Sand Liberals," *Los Angeles Times*, 18 September 2006.

36. Pew Research Center, "Muslims and Islam: Key Findings in the US and around the World," *FactTank*, 22 July 2016, http://www.pewresearch .org/fact-tank/2016/07/22/muslims-and-islam-key-findings-in-the-u-s-and -around-the-world/ (accessed 27 July 2016).

37. Luke Bretherton, "Filters, Fences or Faces: Asylum Seekers and the Moral Status of Borders," ABC Religion & Ethics blog, 28 June 2012, http:// www.abc.net.au/religion/articles/2012/06/28/3535073.htm (accessed 19 October 2017).

38. Ibid.

39. Andrew Sullivan, "The Issue That Could Lose the Next Election for the Democrats," *New York Magazine*, 20 October 2017.

40. Matthew Bolton, *How to Resist: Turn Protest to Power* (London: Bloomsbury, 2017), 73.

41. Pope Francis, *Laudato Sí: On Care for Our Common Home*, 24 May 2015, http://w2.vatican.va/content/francesco/en/encyclicals/documents/papa -francesco_20150524_enciclica-laudato-si.html (accessed 13 August 2018), 147 and 150.

CHAPTER 6   Engaging the Theoretical Debate II

1. Jeffrey Stout, *Democracy and Tradition* (Princeton, NJ: Princeton University Press, 2004), 296–97.

2. Stanley Hauerwas, "Reforming Christian Social Ethics: Ten Theses," in John Berkman and Michael Cartwright, eds., *The Hauerwas Reader* (Durham, NC: Duke University Press, 1981), 111–15.

3. Stout, *Democracy and Tradition*, 138.

4. Quoted in Romand Coles, "Democracy, Theology and the Question of Excess: A Review of Jeffrey Stout's *Democracy and Tradition*," *Modern Theology* 23 (2–5): 312.

5. See especially chapter 15 of MacIntyre's *After Virtue: A Study in Moral Theory* (London: Duckworth Books, 1981) and Chapters XVIII to XX of *Whose Justice? Which Rationality?* (London: Duckworth Books, 1988).

6. Stout, *Democracy and Tradition*, 296.

7. Ibid., 297.

8. Ruth Braunstein, *Prophets and Patriots: Faith in Democracy across the Political Divide* (Oakland: University of California Press, 2017). The community organizing group she studies is part of PICO (People Improving Communities through Organizing) rather than IAF, but it draws on a very similar methodology, with roots in Alinsky.

9. Ibid., 9.

10. Ibid., 56.

11. Ibid., 97–98.

12. Ibid., 148–49.

13. Laura Grattan, *Populism's Power: Radical Grassroots Democracy in America* (New York: Oxford University Press, 2016), 144–45.

14. Ibid., 10.

15. Ibid., 50.

16. Catherine McNichol Stock, *Rural Radicals: From Bacon's Rebellion to the Oklahoma City Bombing* (New York: Penguin, 1997), 55, cited in Grattan, *Populism's Power*, 60.

17. Stock, *Rural Radicals*, 55.

18. Grattan, *Populism's Power*, 159.

19. Saul Alinsky, *Reveille for Radicals* (New York: Vintage Books, 1969), 6, quoted in Luke Bretherton, *Resurrecting Democracy: Faith, Citizenship and the Politics of a Common Life* (New York: Cambridge University Press, 2015), 52.

20. Sheldon Wolin, *Politics and Vision: Continuity and Innovation in Western Political Thought* (Princeton, NJ: Princeton University Press, 2004), 604–5.

21. Ibid., 604.

CHAPTER 7   Inclusive Populism and the Renewal of Politics

1. Chantal Mouffe, *On the Political: Thinking in Action* (London: Routledge, 2005), 54.

2. Luke Bretherton, "Can Politics Be Saved?: Rethinking Church and State," ABC Religion and Ethics blog, 27 September 2010, http://www.abc.net.au/religion/articles/2010/09/27/3023009.htm (accessed 20 February 2015).

3. This legislative change was won, in large part, by Citizens UK's "Just Money" campaign and Archbishop Justin Welby's declaration of a "War on Wonga"—distinct but complementary campaigns that both had the Church at their heart. Others who were vocal supporters of change included East London Labour MP Stella Creasy.

4. Jeffrey Stout, *Blessed are the Organized: Grassroots Democracy in America* (Princeton, NJ: Princeton University Press, 2010), 243.

5. Anna Rowlands, "Pope Francis, *Evangelii Gaudium* and Community Organising," in Dunstan Rodrigues, ed., *Realities Are Greater than Ideas: Evangelisation, Catholicism and Community Organising* (London: Centre for Theology and Community, 2018), 48.

6. Pope Francis, Speech to the Second World Meeting of Popular Movements, Santa Cruz de la Sierra, 9 July 2015, http://w2.vatican.va/content /francesco/en/speeches/2015/july/documents/papa-francesco_20150709 _bolivia-movimenti-popolari.html (accessed 30 June 2017).

7. Angus Ritchie, "Christianity in British Public Life: The Challenges of Pluralism and the Limits of Secularity," ABC Religion and Ethics blog, 21 December 2015, http://www.abc.net.au/religion/articles/2015/12/21/43765 16.htm (accessed 10 January 2018).

8. Ken Briggs, "The Pope's Brilliant Quip," *National Catholic Reporter*, 19 February 2016.

9. Organizers trained by IAF and Citizens UK are involved in alliances in at least six other Western democracies (Australia, Canada, Denmark, France, Germany, and Sweden) and in the unique context of the Hong Kong Special Administrative Region of China.

BIBLIOGRAPHY

Ali, Ruhana, Lina Jamoul, and Yusufi Vali, eds. *A New Covenant of Virtue: Islam and Community Organising*. London: Citizens UK, 2012.

Alinsky, Saul. *Reveille for Radicals*. New York: Vintage Books, 1969.

———. *Rules for Radicals: A Pragmatic Primer for Realistic Radicals*. New York: Random House, 1971.

Barclay, David. *Making Multiculturalism Work: Building Relationships across Deep Difference*. London: Theos, 2013.

Benedict XVI. *Caritas in Veritate*. 2009. http://vatican.va/content/benedict -xvi/en/encyclicals/documents/hf_ben-xvi_enc_20090629_caritas-in -veritate.html.

Berkman, John, and Michael Cartwright, eds. *The Hauerwas Reader*. Durham, NC: Duke University Press, 1981.

Bolton, Matthew. *How to Resist: Turn Protest to Power*. London: Bloomsbury, 2017.

Boyte, Harry. *Everyday Politics: Reconnecting Citizens and Public Life*. Philadelphia: University of Pennsylvania Press, 2004.

Braunstein, Ruth. *Prophets and Patriots: Faith in Democracy across the Political Divide*. Oakland: University of California Press, 2017.

Bretherton, Luke. *Christianity and Contemporary Politics: The Conditions and Possibilities of Faithful Witness*. Oxford: Wiley-Blackwell, 2010.

———. *Resurrecting Democracy: Faith, Citizenship and the Politics of a Common Life*. New York: Cambridge University Press, 2015.

Brown, Peter. *Power and Persuasion in Late Antiquity: Towards a Christian Empire*. Madison: University of Wisconsin Press, 1992.

Burbridge, Caitlin. *Faith and the Politics of "Other": Community Organising amongst London's Congolese Diaspora*. London: Contextual Theology Centre, 2013.

Cavanaugh, William. *Theopolitical Imagination: Discovering the Liturgy as a Political Act in an Age of Global Consumerism*. Edinburgh: T&T Clark, 2002.

Centre for Theology and Community and Citizens UK. Congregational Development Action Learning Community Handbook. Unpublished, 2014.

Church Urban Fund. *Faithful Representation: Faith Representatives on Local
Public Partnerships*. London: Church Urban Fund, 2006.

Citizens Commission on Islam, Participation & Public Life. *The Missing Muslims: Unlocking British Muslim Potential for the Benefit of All*. London:
Citizens UK, 2017.

Commission on Religion and Belief in British Public Life. *Living with Difference: The Report of the Commission on Religion and Belief in British Public
Life*. Cambridge: Woolf Institute, 2015.

Conder, Tim, and Dan Rhodes. *Organizing Church: Grassroots Practices for
Embodying Change in Your Congregation, Your Community, and Our World*.
St. Louis: Chalice Press, 2017.

Coulson, Andrea B., and James Bonner, *Living Wage Employers: Evidence of
UK Business Cases*. Glasgow: University of Strathclyde, 2015, https://www
.livingwage.org.uk/news/new-evidence-business-case-adopting-living
-wage.

Cox, Harvey. *The Secular City: Secularization and Urbanization (A Theological
Perspective)*. New York: MacMillan, 1965.

Deneen, Patrick. *Why Liberalism Failed*. New Haven, CT: Yale University
Press, 2018.

Dinham, Adam, Robert Furbey, and Vivien Lowndes, eds., *Faith in the Public
Realm: Controversies, Policies and Practices*. London: Policy Press, 2009.

Doering, Bernard, ed. *The Philosopher and the Provocateur: The Correspondence of
Jacques Maritain and Saul Alinsky*. Notre Dame, IN: University of Notre
Dame Press, 1994.

Francis. *Evangelii Gaudium: Apostolic Exhortation on the Proclamation of the
Gospel in Today's World*. 2013. http://w2.vatican.va/content/francesco
/en/apost_exhortations/documents/papa-francesco_esortazione-ap
_20131124_evangelii-gaudium.html.

———. *Laudato Sí: On Care for our Common Home*. 2015. http://w2.vatican.va
/content/francesco/en/encyclicals/documents/papa-francesco_20150524
_enciclica-laudato-si.html.

Gecan, Michael. *Going Public: An Organizer's Guide to Citizen Action*. Boston:
Beacon Press, 2002.

———. *Effective Organising for Congregational Renewal*. Chicago: ACTA Publications, 2008.

Grattan, Laura. *Populism's Power: Radical Grassroots Democracy in America*.
New York: Oxford University Press, 2016.

Green, Beth, Angus Ritchie, and Tim Thorlby. *Church Growth in East London:
A Grassroots View*. London: Centre for Theology and Community, 2016.

Horton, John, and Susan Mendus, eds. *After MacIntyre: Critical Perspectives on the Work of Alasdair MacIntyre*. Notre Dame, IN: University of Notre Dame Press, 1994.

Hursthouse, Rosalind, Gavin Lawrence, and Warren Quinn, eds. *Virtues and Reasons: Philippa Foot and Moral Theory*. Oxford: Clarendon Press, 1996.

International Centre for the Study of Radicalisation and Political Violence. *Recruitment and Mobilisation for the Islamist Militant Movement in Europe*. London, 2007.

Ivereigh, Austen. *The Great Reformer: Francis and the Making of a Radical Pope*. London: Allen and Unwin, 2014.

Jiménez, Tomás. *Immigrants in the United States: How Well Are They Integrating into Society?* Washington, DC: Migration Policy Institute, 2011.

Lilla, Mark. *The Once and Future Liberal: After Identity Politics*. New York: HarperCollins, 2017.

Luciani, Rafael. *Pope Francis and the Theology of the People*. New York: Orbis Books, 2017.

MacIntyre, Alasdair. *After Virtue: A Study in Moral Theory*. London: Duckworth Books, 1981.

———. *Whose Justice? Which Rationality?* London: Duckworth Books, 1988.

MacLeod, Jay. *Community Organising: A Practical and Theological Evaluation*. London: Christian Action, 1993.

Milbank, John, and Adrian Pabst. *The Politics of Virtue: Post-Liberalism and the Human Future*. London: Rowman and Littlefield, 2016.

Mouffe, Chantal. *On the Political: Thinking in Action*. London: Routledge, 2005.

———. *Agonistics: Thinking the World Politically*. London: Verso, 2013.

Nozick, Robert. *Anarchy, State and Utopia*. New York: Basic Books, 1974.

Obama, Barack. *Dreams from My Father: A Story of Race and Inheritance*. New York: Three Rivers Press, 2004.

Organized Communities, Stronger Schools: Impact of Community and Youth Organizing on Public School Reform. Providence, RI: Annenberg Institute for School Reform, Brown University, May 2009.

Owen, David. *Ethnic Minorities in Great Britain: Patterns of Population Change, 1981–91*. Warwick, UK: University of Warwick Centre for Research in Ethnic Relations, 1995.

Polanyi, Karl. *The Great Transformation*. Boston: First Beacon, 1957.

Putnam, Robert. *Bowling Alone: The Collapse and Revival of American Community*. New York: Simon and Schuster, 2000.

Rawls, John. *A Theory of Justice*. Oxford: Oxford University Press, 1971.

———. *Political Liberalism*. New York: Columbia University Press, 1993.

———. *The Law of Peoples*. Cambridge, MA: Harvard University Press, 1999.

Ritchie, Angus. *From Morality to Metaphysics: The Theistic Implications of Our Ethical Commitments.* (Oxford: Oxford University Press, 2012).

———, ed. *Crunch Time: A Call to Action* (London: Contextual Theology Centre, 2010).

Ritchie, Angus, and David Barclay, eds. *God and the Moneylenders: Faith and the Battle against Exploitative Lending.* London: Contextual Theology Centre, 2013.

Rodrigues, Dunstan, ed. *Realities Are Greater than Ideas: Evangelisation, Catholicism and Community Organising.* London: Centre for Theology and Community, 2018.

Rogers, Mary Beth. *Cold Anger: A Story of Faith and Power Politics.* Denton: University of North Texas Press, 1990.

Saggar, Shamit, and Will Somerville. *Building a British Model of Integration in an Era of Immigration: Policy Lessons for Government.* Washington, DC: Migration Policy Institute, 2012.

Sennett, Richard. *The Corrosion of Character: The Personal Consequences of Work in the New Capitalism.* New York: W. W. Norton, 1998.

Shanahan, Chris. *A Theology of Community Organising: Power to the People.* London: Routledge, 2013.

Siedentop, Larry. *Inventing the Individual: The Origins of Western Liberalism.* London: Allen Lane, 2014.

Social Integration Commission. *Kingdom United: Thirteen Steps to Tackle Social Segregation.* London: Social Integration Commission, 2014.

Stock, Catherine McNichol. *Rural Radicals: From Bacon's Rebellion to the Oklahoma City Bombing.* New York: Penguin, 1997.

Stout, Jeffrey. *Democracy and Tradition.* Princeton, NJ: Princeton University Press, 2009.

———. *Blessed Are the Organized: Grassroots Democracy in America.* Princeton, NJ: Princeton University Press, 2010.

Thorlby, Tim. *Love, Sweat and Tears: Church Planting in East London.* London: Centre for Theology and Community, 2015.

———. *A Time to Sow: Anglican Catholic Church Growth in London.* London: Centre for Theology and Community, 2017.

Walton, Andy. *Is There a Religious Right in Britain?* London: Theos, 2013.

Wolin, Sheldon. *Tocqueville between Two Worlds: The Making of a Political and Theoretical Life.* Princeton, NJ: Princeton University Press, 2001.

———. *Politics and Vision: Continuity and Innovation in Western Political Thought.* Princeton, NJ: Princeton University Press, 2004.

INDEX

abortion, 75–76, 100–102
Achola, Lucy, 43–44
Acton, Lord, 30
Affordable Care Act, 47
affordable housing campaigns
  Community Land Trust, 33, 98–99,
    116, 134
  East London Mosque participation
    in, 38
  impact on integration, 116
  of London Citizens, 29, 98–99
  Manor Park parish participation in,
    43–44
  Nehemiah Housing, 46, 134
  role of religious institutions in, 116,
    149
African American population, 83, 117,
  143
After Virtue (MacIntyre), 139
agency
  in community organizing, 35
  in inclusive populism, 4
  lacking in fake populism, 5
  in liberalism, 10
  in populism of Pope Francis, 18–19
  in voluntarism, 63–64
Alfonso, Father, 47
Ali, Ruhana, x
Alinsky, Saul, 28, 144
  concerns regarding teaching of, 69–70
  on financial independence, 33–34
  founding the IAF, 5, 158n3
  on grassroots organizing, 84
  impacts on populism, 140

instrumentalizing institutions, 45
leadership development of, 41
on self-interest, 36, 76–77, 78
use of tension, 31–32
on wedge issues, 99
"Alliance Schools" program, 56, 115
Anthony (Zimbabwean asylum seeker),
  40–41
antipolitical populism, 5, 71–72
anti-usury law campaigns, 93–96, 100,
  149
Aristotle, 153

Bachelard, Sarah, 96, 99
Bannon, Steve, 117
Barclay, David, x, 15, 51, 72–74, 91–92,
  122, 125, 144, 149, 152, 164n35
Bari, Muhammad Abdul, 94
Barking and Dagenham (London
  borough), 113–16
Benedict XVI (pope), 93
"Big Society" program, 85–87
"birther" movement, 82
Blair, Tony, 1, 9, 86, 118
Blessed Are the Organized (Stout), 119
B'nai Jehoshua Beth Elohim (BJBE),
  Congregation, 47–49
BNP (British National Party), 114
Bolton, Matthew, 40–41
Bond, John, 32, 42
Booth, Catherine, 108
Booth, William, 108
Boyte, Harry, 21
Braunstein, Ruth, 140–41, 142, 167n8

Brazilian diaspora, 113
Bretherton, Luke, 5, 70, 71–72, 94–95,
    129, 130, 131, 156n9
Brexit, 1, 2, 16, 114, 116, 122, 165n13
British Humanist Association, 152
British National Party (BNP), 114
Brown, Gordon, 85, 87
Brown, Peter, 66
BUILD (Baltimoreans United In
    Leadership Development), 46
Bunting, Madeline, 85, 86
Burbridge, Caitlin, x, 111–12, 120

Caesar, Pearl, 53
Cameron, David, 84, 85–87
Caritas in Veritate (Pope Benedict XVI),
    93
Casey, Robert P., 75
Cavanaugh, William, 156–57n20
CDSP (Church Divinity School of the
    Pacific), 30–31
Centre for Theology and Community
    (CTC), x, 53, 91, 97
Chambers, Ed, 28, 36, 45, 77
child detention, 46, 110
Chinn, Trevor, 166n26
Chowdhury, Sotez, 114–15, 165n14
Christianity
    declines in practice, 7–8
    in global migration, 2–3, 6
    inadequate representation of women
        in, 164n47
    in liberalism's history, 63
    misconceptions of immigration's im-
        pact on, 7–8, 122
    in a pluralist society, 27–28, 138–39
    populist visions in, 65–67, 138
    in right-wing populism, 2, 8–9
    similarities to other faiths, 99
    usury teachings in, 24, 93–96
    See also churches
"Christian populism," 65–67, 138
Church Divinity School of the Pacific
    (CDSP), 30–31
churches
    impact on relationships, 20

    in Living Wage campaigns, 12
    role in democracies, 11, 19–20
    traditions embodied in, 139
    transforming self-interest, 37
    and wedge issues, 100
    See also Christianity; religious
        institutions
Church Urban Fund survey, 50
citizens
    in antipolitical populism, 71–72
    community organizing's challenge to,
        153–54
    convictions of, 3–4
    in inclusive populism, 3, 58
    in liberalism, 10, 156n20
    in political populism, 70–71
    role of institutions in forming, ix,
        19–21, 71
    See also agency
Citizens UK
    accomplishments of, 46
    accountability assemblies, 85, 87
    the "Big Society" program and,
        85–87
    "CitySafe" campaign, 49–50, 112–13
    the Congolese diaspora and, 110–13
    economic inequalities addressed by,
        150–51
    financial independence of, 34, 85–86
    the IAF and, x, 5, 158n3
    inclusive approach of, 51, 72, 73–74,
        122
    integrating spirituality, 97
    integration approach of, 110–13
    international impact of, 169n9
    "Just Money" campaign, 168n3
    Living Wage campaign, 46, 134
    membership dues, 34, 88
    The Missing Muslims, 123–25, 166n26
    mutual witnessing in, 49
    pluralism of, 91–92
    political populism of, 70–71
    secular members, 50–51
    "Strangers into Citizens" campaign,
        132–33
    strengthening institutions, 91

training in relational meetings, 36
and wedge issues, 75–76, 99–100, 102
See also London Citizens; TELCO
"CitySafe" campaign, 49–50, 112–13
Clegg, Nick, 75, 87
Clifton, John, 165n13
Clinton, Bill, 1, 81
Clinton, Hillary, 13, 69, 75, 82–83, 118
Coates, Ta-Nehisi, 81–82
Coke, Nick, 165n13
Cold Anger (Rogers), 77
Community Land Trust campaigns, 33,
    98–99, 116, 134
community organizing
    "bottom-up" approach, 85
    challenges offered by, 151–54
    compromise in, 17, 19, 40–41, 71,
        100, 152
    concerns regarding desirability of,
        70–80
    concerns regarding effectiveness of,
        81–92
    conversation registers in, 24–25
    criticisms of, 69–70
    embodying inclusive populism, ix, 4,
        5, 28
    embodying negotiated pluralism,
        23–25, 80
    encouraging diverse *convictions*, 59
    importance of self-interest, 22,
        35–41, 58
    inclusiveness of, 21–22, 141, 142
    as institution-based, 19–21, 141, 142
    leadership development in, 41–45
    plurality of motivations in, 45–51
    politicians' roles in, 29, 81–88, 102,
        147
    redistribution of power in, 28–31
    self-correcting dynamic within, 90,
        91, 102–3
    and spirituality, 96–99
    steps involved in, 33, 41–42
    strengthening institutions, 52–56, 58,
        66
    tension used in, 31–33
    wedge issues in, 75–76, 99–102, 132

ComRes (opinion pollster), 109
Conant, Vanessa, 37
Conder, Tim, 30, 31, 52–53
Congolese diaspora, x, 109–13
Congregational Development Learning
    Community, 91
Congregation B'nai Jehoshua Beth
    Elohim (BJBE), 47–49
Connolly, Sean, 42–44, 90
conversation registers, 24–25, 100–101,
    108, 139
convictions
    in community organizing, 59
    defined, 3–4
    liberalism's understanding of, 11–13,
        59–60
    in public life, 7
    role in politics, 4, 10–13
    in traditionalism, 137–39
    See also religion; values
CoRAB (Commission on Religion and
    Belief in British Public Life), 3–4,
    108, 121
Corbyn, Jeremy, 13, 16
Cortés, Ernesto, 19, 42, 52, 58, 66, 77,
    90, 91
Coulter, Ann, 69
Cox, Harvey, 2–3
Creasy, Stella, 168n3
CTC (Centre for Theology and
    Community), x, 53, 91, 97

Da'esh, 128
Daniel (Citizens UK organizer), 38
debate (conversation register), 24, 49,
    100, 139
democracy
    and antipolitical populism, 71–72
    grassroots organizing in, 84
    plurality necessary in, 10
    and political populism, 70–71
    popular leadership necessary to, 151
    role of civil institutions in, 11–12, 14,
        19–20, 66–67, 71
    role of community organizing in,
        144–45

democracy (*continued*)
Tocqueville's views on, 64–65
untidiness of, 25–26
Democracy and Tradition (Stout), 137,
139–40
Democratic Party
exclusionary approach of, 75
progressive identity politics of, 118
and Trump's election victory, 82–83
and Trump's fake populism, 147–48
Deneen, Patrick, 64–65
desire, 64–65, 66
Dhaliwal, Sukhwant, 72
Dinham, Adam, 50
divine will, 63–64
Donovan, Judy, 53
Dummett, Michael, 130

early Church, 66, 94
East Brooklyn Congregations (IAF
affiliate), 46, 134
East London Citizens Organisation,
The. *See* TELCO
East London Mosque, 38–40, 73–74,
119, 123
economy (market)
inequalities in, 150–51
and integration policy, 120
power of, 12–13, 14, 144
relationships resisting commodification in, 149–51
and rise of far-right populism, 3, 148
in secularizing liberalism, 92
*Effective Organising for Congregational
Renewal* (Gecan), xi
elections
2010 UK general, 85, 87
2016 UK London mayoral, 27–28
2016 US presidential, 13, 116
2017 UK general, 13, 16
Elliott, Larry, 16
English, Prayer, Action congregation,
113
ethno-religious identity, 121
European Union referendum, 1, 16,
114, 116, 122

evaluation, 45, 54
Evangelical Alliance, 109
Evangelii Gaudium (Pope Francis), 18,
89
exclusion
and extremism, 126–28
by the liberal left, 15–16, 75
and motivation, 51
of Muslim communities, 124
of the poorer communities, 152
of regressive groups, 72–76
in theology of Chris Shanahan, 80
in Tea Party populism, 141
extremism
anxieties concerning, 127
exposing flaws of liberalism, 9
and hostility toward Muslims, 122
and isolation, 15, 20, 72–74
legislation addressing, 106
and mosques, 125–27
radicalization process, 20, 126–28
and regressive groups, 72–76
relationships as defense against, 21,
71, 74, 127
and rise of far-right populism, 148

fake populisms
factors in rise of, 147–48
liberalism's role in rise of, ix, 62
role of citizens in, 5
traditions in, 140
of Trump, 142, 147–48, 150
See also left-wing populism; right-
wing populism
Farage, Nigel, 9, 116
financial crises, 3, 9, 14, 83, 93, 148
financial independence
of Citizens UK, 34, 85–86
in community organizing, 33–35,
141, 142
and funding sources, 88
of the IAF, 34
of the Tea Party movement, 142
of TELCO, 90
Firth, Dan, 114–15, 165n14
"flawed civil society" approach, 21

Francis (pope)
acts of *ressourcement*, 66
Evangelii Gaudium, 89
on human ecology needs, 134, 135
Laudato Sí, 134
as political figure, 153
on power in the Church, 101,
164n47
on various populisms, 4–5
vision for the poorest, xi, 18–19,
97–98, 151
FreedomWorks (organization), 140

Gecan, Michael, 37, 77, 91
Gethner, Judith, 48
Goldsmith, Zac, 27, 28, 32–33
good, conceptions of
and *convictions*, 11–12
the economy and, 93
in liberalism, 10, 59, 106–7
and liberty, 60, 64
in moral realism, 61–62
in negotiated pluralism, 45–51,
107–8, 130–31
through negotiation, 17, 19, 24–25,
152
Rawls's views on, 59, 60–62
role of mediating institutions in, 66,
151
in secularizing liberalism, 11, 60–62
Tea Party's views on, 141
Gove, Michael, 106
Grattan, Laura, 13, 141, 142–44
Greater Boston Interfaith Organization, 46–47
Grieve, Dominic, 166n26
Guardian, 93, 101

Haste, Andy, 94
Hauerwas, Stanley, 137, 138–39
health care reform, 46–47, 83
Heinemeier, John, 53
hijab, 122, 123
Hill, Peter, 29
Hong Kong and Shanghai Banking
Corporation (HSBC), 32, 42

Hoo, Robert, 30–31
housing
and immigration concerns, 8–9, 16,
133–34
and integration policy, 120
See also affordable housing campaigns
HSBC (Hong Kong and Shanghai
Banking Corporation), 32, 42
human will, 64
Hurricane Katrina, 119

IAF. *See* Industrial Areas Foundation
identity politics, 118
immigration
anxieties concerning, 1, 8–9, 16,
114–15
blamed for dilution of Christianity,
122
border conceptions, 129–30
community organizing's approach to,
132–34, 135
Muslim immigration, 8–9, 116–17,
120–22
the New Citizens Legal Service and,
110
policies discouraging, 6
in political liberalism, 129–31
process of policy formation, 131–32
in right-wing populism, 2, 116–17
See also integration; migrant communities; migration (global)
inclusion
of community organizing, 21–22,
79–80
in Interfaith, 141
and left-wing populism, 15–16
linguistic and cultural barriers to, 111
and regressive groups, 72–76
inclusive populism
as antidote to current defects, 147–49
contrasted with secularizing liberalism, 3
economic inequalities addressed by,
150–51
embodied by community organizing,
4, 5, 18, 28, 58

inclusive populism (*continued*)
  emergence of, 154
  relationships in, 58, 71
  role of *convictions* in, 4
  role of institutions in, ix, 58, 149
  traditions needed in, ix, 58, 140
individualism, 10, 65, 141
Industrial Areas Foundation (IAF)
  accomplishments of, 46–47
  "Alliance Schools" program, 56, 115
  under Chambers, 36, 45, 77
  conception of self-interest, 77
  economic inequalities addressed by, 150–51
  financial independence of, 34
  founding of, 5, 28, 158n3
  impact of, 118–19, 169n9
  membership dues, 34, 88
  political populism of, 70–71
  relationship to Citizens UK, x
  Rio Grande *colonias* campaign, 34–35, 46
  strengthening institutions, 52
  training in relational meetings, 36
  training on issue of power, 30–31
  and wedge issues, 75–76, 99–100, 102
institutions, mediating civil society
  in antipolitical populism, 71–72
  community organizing's challenge to, 153
  diversity in, 46
  far-left populist views of, 14–15
  in political populism, 70–71
  political roles of, 152–53
  relational tests of, 73
  relationships built through, 17
  role in community organizing, 19–21, 23, 52–56, 58, 88
  role in democracy, ix, 11–12, 14, 19–20, 66–67, 71, 144, 151
  role in inclusive populism, ix, 23, 149
  role in the People's Party, 142–43
  in secularizing liberalism, 92
  traditions embodied in, 139
  undermined by liberalism, 148

  and wedge issues, 100–101
  in white working class communities, 115
integration
  and African Americans, 117
  and American racial tensions, 116–17
  Barking and Dagenham example, 113–16
  Congolese diaspora example, 109–13
  and far-right populism, 117–18
  impacts of community organizing on, 118–20, 128–29
  and Islam, 120–29
  liberal coercive policies, 106–7, 108, 113–14
  and Muslim women, 122–25
  in negotiated pluralism, 108–9
  obstacles to, 111–12
  perspectives of the marginalized, 135
  policy formulation considerations, 119–20
  values in policy, 105–7
  See also immigration
Interfaith (organizing alliance), 140, 141
International Centre for the Study of Radicalisation and Political Violence, 20, 126
International Monetary Fund briefing, 6
Inventing the Individual (Siedentop), 63
Islam
  anxieties concerning, 8–9, 74
  ethno-religious identities in, 121
  and extremism, 125–29
  in global migration, 2–3, 6
  and integration, 120–29
  in a pluralist society, 27–28
  in public life, 7
  right-wing populism on, 2, 8–9
  similarities to other faiths, 99
  usury teachings in, 24, 93–96
  and women's leadership, 122–25
  See also mosques; Muslim communities
Ivereigh, Austin, 97

Jameson, Neil, 124, 158n3
Jamoul, Lina, 56–58, 123
Jeraj, Sarfraz, 38
Jeremiah alliance, 119
Jeremy (Congolese migrant), 112–13
Jiménez, Tomás, 120
jobs and wages
    anxieties regarding, 8–9, 16, 114–15
    among global migrants, 6
    and immigration policy, 133–34
    and integration policy, 120
    and Muslim women, 125
    See also Living Wage campaigns
Johnson, Boris, 87
Judaism, 27–28, 47–49, 99. See also
    synagogues
"justice as fairness" framework, 60–61
"Just Money" campaign, 168n3

Kedar, Karyn, 47
Keystone Pipeline, 142
Khan, Dilowar, 38–40, 49, 119
Khan, Sadiq, 27, 32–33, 158n1
KPMG (accounting firm), 78

Labour Party, 9, 16, 85
Latin American communities, 83, 117
Laudato Sí (Pope Francis), 134
leadership development
    in community organizing, 41–45
    maintaining a sustainable pace in, 44,
        54–55, 89–90
    of Muslim women, 122–25
    self-interest in, 56–58
    and wedge issues, 100
left-wing populism
    community organizing's challenge to,
        151–52
    detached idealism of, 18, 40
    expressed through political parties,
        22
    on immigration, 131, 132
    liberalism's role in rise of, ix
    progressive tests of, 21, 74–75
    traditions in, 140
    weaknesses of, 3, 13–18

Le Pen, Marine, 2, 9
liberalism
    benefits of, 139
    coercive integration policies, 106–7,
        108, 113–14
    convictions removed from, 4
    defined, 4
    and economic inequality, 150
    expressed through political parties, 22
    false neutrality of, 62, 122
    and immigration policy, 129–31
    of Nozick, 10, 59
    of Rawls, 10, 60–62
    and religious identity, 121
    and rise of right-wing populism, 2,
        9–13
    role of Christianity in, 63
    theoretical debates on, 59–67
    weaknesses of, 10–13, 25, 131,
        148–49
    See also secularizing liberalism
liberty, 14, 60, 63, 64, 66
Lilla, Mark, 74–76, 118
Linder, John, 47–48
Livingstone, Ken, 27, 28, 33, 86
Living Wage campaigns
    of BUILD, 46
    of Citizens UK, 42, 46
    impacts of, 134
    "Local Jobs for Local People" cam-
        paign, 38
    of London Citizens, 29, 32, 42, 87
    during the London Olympics, 41
    role of religious institutions in, 12,
        149
    of TELCO, 12, 77–78
Locality (charity organization), 86
"Local Jobs for Local People" cam-
    paign, 38
Local Public Partnerships, 50
London Citizens
    accountability assemblies, 27–28, 29,
        32–33, 34, 45, 71, 87
    anti-usury campaign, 93–96, 100, 149
    Community Land Trust campaigns,
        33, 98–99

London Citizens (*continued*)
  CTC's work with, 53
  founding members of, 39
  letters of understanding in, 73
  Living Wage campaigns, 29, 32, 42, 87
  membership dues, 34
  and Muslim financial services campaigns, 94–96
  Olympics campaign, 41
  power of, 29, 34
  "Strangers into Citizens" campaign, 40–41
  strengthening institutions, 91
  See also Citizens UK
London East Academy, 39
London Muslim Centre, 38–40, 119
Luciani, Rafael, 97–98

MacIntyre, Alasdair, 10, 129–30, 131, 137, 138–39, 148
MacLeod, Jay, 28, 77
Macron, Emmanuel, 2
Manor Park parish, 42–44, 90
Maritain, Jacques, 76
market. *See* economy (market)
McDermott, Matt, 47–49
"Meals on Heels" program, 123
media coverage, 21, 33, 35
membership dues, 34–35, 88
middle class
  in Latin America, 97–98
  in the Occupy movement, 13, 80, 144
  and the perspectives of the poorest, 135
  power of, 31
  progressive left support in, 152
migrant communities
  commonalities of, 148–49
  jobs and wages in, 6
  politicians problematizing, 23
  in public life, 6–7
  religion in, 15–16
  See also immigration; integration
migration (global)
  changing patterns of, 5–7
  exposing flaws of liberalism, 9
  impact on Christianity, 7–8

religion in, 2–3, 6
and rise of right-wing populism, 2–3, 8, 148
  See also immigration; integration
Milbank, Arabella, x
Milbank, John, 63, 64
Missing Muslims, The (Citizens UK), 123–25
Mizen, Barry, 112
Mizen, Jimmy, 112
Mizen, Margaret, 112
moral constructivism, 61–62, 160n4
moral realism, 61–62, 160n4
Mosque Foundation (Chicago), 56–58, 123
mosques
  and extremism, 20, 125–27
  in Living Wage campaigns, 12
  relationships built in, 20
  role in communities, 126–27
  role in democracies, 11, 19–20
  role of women in, 125
  traditions embodied in, 139
  transforming self-interest, 37
  See also religious institutions
motivation
  cynical views of, 76–80
  and exclusivity, 51
  impact of community organizing on, 38–40
  and insincerity, 51
  plurality of, 45–51
  role of values and vocation in, 36–37
  See also self-interest
Mouffe, Chantal, 10, 25, 62, 148
Movement for Reform Judaism (MRJ), 91
Muslimaat (women's group), 123
Muslim communities
  excluded from Tea Party movement, 141
  fear and anxieties surrounding, 8–9, 116–17
  financial services, 94–96
  hostility faced by, 8–9, 122, 123, 125
  and integration, 23, 120–22
  role of mosques in, 126–27

and women's leadership, 122–25
See also Islam
mutual witness (conversation register), 24, 25, 45–46, 49, 55, 95–96,
100, 139

National Secular Society, 152
Native Americans, 117
NCG (Nevadans for the Common
Good), 30–31
NCOT (New Citizens Organizing
Team), 110
negotiated pluralism
anti-usury campaign example, 93–96,
100
conceptions of the good in, 45–51,
130–31
conversation registers in, 24–25,
100–101
embodied by community organizing,
23–25, 80
national values in, 107–9
relationships in, 25
secular traditions in, 51
tradition varieties in, 139–40
negotiation (conversation register),
17, 19, 24–25, 33, 71, 95–96, 100,
139–40, 152
Nehemiah Housing campaign, 46, 134
neutrality, 51, 59–60, 61–62, 92, 122
Nevadans for the Common Good
(NCG), 30–31
New Citizens Legal Service, 110
New Citizens Organizing Team
(NCOT), 110
New Covenant of Virtue, A (Ali, Jamoul,
and Vali), xi
Newham General Hospital, 78, 133
New Hope Lutheran Church (New
York City), 52–53
Newman, Adrian, 93–94
nominalism, 63
Nozick, Robert, 10, 59

"Obama" (Coulter), 69
Obama, Barack, 1, 69, 70, 81–82,
83–84, 117, 132, 147

Oborne, Peter, 166n26
Occupy movement (UK), 14–15,
17, 18, 33, 40, 143–44,
151–52
Occupy movement (US), 13–15,
143–44, 151–52
Ockham, William of, 63
Olympics (London, 2012), 38, 41,
42–43
one-to-one relational meetings, 35–37,
48, 54, 57–58
Organizing for America (community
organizing movement), 83

Pabst, Adrian, 63, 64
paid community organizers, 34, 88–90,
100
Pallavancini, Yayha (imam), 93
Panim El Panim project, 48
Patriots (Tea Party movement), 140,
141–42
Paul (apostle), 63
People Improving Communities
through Organizing (PICO),
167n8
People's Party (US), 142–43
Pew Institute, 101, 128
PICO (People Improving Communities through Organizing),
167n8
pluralism
American history of, 117
convictions articulated in, 4
genuineness of, 91–92
of secular humanism, 152
theoretical debates on, 137–40
traditions in, 137–40
See also negotiated pluralism
Political Liberalism (Rawls), 60
political populism, 5, 70–71
politicians
accountability of, 29
community organizing's challenge to,
152–53
rhetoric on integration, 23
role in community organizing,
81–88, 102, 147

politics
    current mood of anger and anxiety,
        1–3
    identity politics, 118
    impact of *convictions* on, 4
    inclusive populism as antidote to
        defects of, 105, 147–49
    political parties in, 22, 118
    role of *convictions* in, 11–12
    role of mediating institutions in,
        22–23, 152–53
    role of religion in, x
    "top-down" conceptions of, 152
    See also specific approaches
poorest communities
    in Christian populism, 66
    commonalities of, 148–49
    impact of immigration policy on, 131
    the left's failing of, 16–17, 152
    Pope Francis's vision for, xi, 18–19
    redistribution of power to, 28–29
    self-interest of, 40, 134–35
    spirituality of, 97–98
    undermined by liberalism, 12–13, 14,
        148
populism
    antipolitical form, 5, 71–72
    comparisons of, 140–42
    concerns regarding, 70–72
    differing contextual meanings of,
        4–5
    of the People's Party, 142–43
    political form of, 70–71
    popular self-interest in, 40
    role of traditions in, 143–45
    and spirituality, 98
    theoretical debates on, 137–45
    See also fake populisms; inclusive
        populism
Populist Party (US), 143
power
    in antipolitical populism, 71–72
    community organizing mediating,
        55, 111–12, 144–45
    devolution of, 86
    inequalities in, 150

Jesus's teachings on, 99
    within Muslim communities,
        122–23
    of paid organizers, 88–90
    in political populism, 70–71
    redistribution of, 28–31, 101
    in religious institutions, 30–31
    and wedge issues, 100
progressive tests, 15–16, 21, 72–73,
    74–75, 125, 144, 152
Prophets and Patriots (Braunstein), 140
public life
    civil society in, 22–23
    convictions in, 7
    debate on common good in, 10
    migrant communities in, 6–7
    Muslim participation in, 127
    religion in, 7, 11, 50, 121–22
Putin, Vladimir, 2, 9

Quinn, Warren, 64, 161n12

"raceless antiracism," 81–82
racism, 81–82, 117, 119, 162n18
Rawls, John, 10, 59, 60–62, 137, 141,
    160n2, 161n12
realism, 61–62, 160n4
*Recruitment and Mobilisation for the
    Islamist Militant Movement in
    Europe* (ICSRPV), 126
redistributive liberalism (Rawls), 10
relational tests, 21, 73–74
relationships
    built in institutions, 19–20, 149–51
    in community organizing, 21–22,
        35–38
    and extremism, 73–74, 126–28
    impact of community organizing on,
        38–40
    impact of right-wing populism on,
        25–26
    impact on institutions, 54
    and integration, 108–9, 119–20
    and leadership development, 57–58
    mutual witnessing in, 49
    in negotiated pluralism, 25, 107–9

power through, 29
role of Muslim women, 123
and wedge issues, 100
religion
    and *convictions*, 3–4
    and ethnic identity, 121
    and global migration, 2–3, 6
    liberalism's understanding of, 11–13
    and mutual witnessing, 24
    and the nation-state, 156n20
    role in politics, x, 10–13
    role in public life, 7
    and secularization, ix–x
    in secularizing liberalism, 60–62
    solidarity in, 27–28
    spirituality in, 96–99
    See also religious institutions
religious identities, 121
religious institutions
    community organizing's challenge to,
        153
    diverse nature of, 45–46
    hallmarks of organized churches,
        53–56
    in political populism, 70–71
    power in, 30–31
    relational power of, 149–51
    relationships built through, 17
    role in community organizing, 149,
        164n39
    role in democracy, 11–12, 71, 151
    role in politics, 10–13
    in secularizing liberalism, 92
    spirituality in, 96–99
    strengthened through community
        organizing, 52–56
    transforming self-interest, 37
    values of, 77
    in white working class communities,
        115
    See also specific institutions
Resurrecting Democracy (Bretherton), 5,
    156n9
Reveille for Radicals (Alinsky), 76
Rhodes, Dan, 30, 31, 52–53
"Right to Buy" policy, 114–15

right-wing populism
    and economic inequalities, 150
    elite leaders of, 9
    expressed through political parties,
        22
    global commonalities in, 2
    hostility toward immigration, 7–9,
        131
    impact on extremism, 15, 127–28
    and integration, 117–18
    liberalism's role in rise of, ix, 9–13
    and "post-truth" politics, 8–9
    progressive tests of, 74
    racism in rise of, 82
    rhetoric of, 20, 25, 127–28
    rise of, ix, 2–3, 9–13, 16, 74, 105,
        147–48
    spread through media, 21
    the Tea Party movement and, 72, 142
    traditions in, 140
    underlying causes of, ix, 2–3, 9–13,
        82, 105, 147–48
    "us versus them" dichotomy in, 117,
        124
    weaknesses of, 3
Rio Grande *colonias* campaign, 34–35,
    46
Rogers, Mary Beth, 77
roll call, 34
Roman Empire, 66
Romney, Mitt, 46, 83
Rougeau, Vincent, 95
Rowlands, Anna, 151
Rubin, Robert, 83
Rules for Radicals (Alinsky), 69
Russia, 1, 2, 3

Saggar, Shamit, 106
Said, Jamal (imam), 57
Sanders, Bernie, 13, 81
Saudi Arabia, 9
schools (mediating civil institutions)
    "Alliance Schools" program, 56, 115
    community organizing's challenge to,
        153
    diversity in, 46

schools (*continued*)
  role in democracies, 11, 71
  school reform, 36
  strengthened through community
    organizing, 56
Secular City, The (Cox), 2–3
Secular Humanism
  in community organizing, 12, 23–24,
    99–100
  community organizing's challenge to,
    152
  as substantive tradition, 152, 157n24
secularization, ix–x, 3, 6, 8
secularizing liberalism
  compared to inclusive populism, 3, 21
  conceptions of good in, 144
  convictions in, 4
  defined, 4, 59
  disempowering the poorest, 12–13
  false neutrality of, 59–60, 92, 122
  and "flawed civil society" approach,
    21
  negative impacts of, 58, 66, 140
  Rawls's defense of, 60–62
  regarding religion as divisive, 11,
    19–20
  the rise of right-wing populism and,
    ix, 10–13
  Siedentop's assessment of, 63
  undermining liberty, 60
  weaknesses in, ix, 10–13
self-interest
  in community organizing, 35–41
  criticized as cynical, 76–80
  defined, 35–36
  IAF's conception of, 77
  and integration, 110, 112
  in leadership development, 56–58
  of Muslim women, 123
  in negotiated pluralism, 80
  and pragmatic compromise, 40–41
  questions identifying, 36
  role in congregational renewal, 37–38
  and wedge issues, 100
  in white working class communities,
    115–16

See also motivation
Shanahan, Chris, 78–80
Siedentop, Larry, 63, 65, 140
Singer, Peter, 130
Singer, Renata, 130
slavery, 117
"small-state" liberalism (Nozick), 10, 59
Social Integration Commission, 20
Somerville, Will, 106
Southall Black Sisters, 72
spirituality, 54, 96–99
St. Antony's Catholic Church (Forest
  Gate), 32
state (government)
  in community organizing, 22, 85–88,
    144
  devolving power, 86
  differing notions of, 111
  and individualism, 64–65
  instrumentalizing institutions, 20–21
  and integration, 23
  liberal views of, 130
  loyalty demanded by, 156–57n20
  power of, 12–13, 144
  in secularizing liberalism, 92
Stepney Fathers Group, 129
St. George-in-the-East (Shadwell),
  98–99, 113, 123
Stiglitz, Joseph, 83
St. Joseph the Worker (McAllen, TX),
  47
Stout, Jeffrey, 34–35, 47, 52, 83–84, 90,
  119, 137, 138, 139–40, 150
"Strangers into Citizens" campaign,
  40–41, 132–33
student unions (mediating civil institutions), 46, 50, 100
Sullivan, Andrew, 132
Summers, Lawrence, 83
synagogues
  renewed through organizing,
    47–49
  role in democracies, 11, 19–20
  traditions embodied in, 139
  transforming self-interest, 37
  See also religious institutions

Taylor, Gerald, 52–53
Tea Party movement, 72, 140–42, 143
TELCO (The East London Citizens
    Organisation), x
    Barking and Dagenham case study,
        115–16
    and Brexit, 165n13
    "CitySafe" campaign, 49–50, 112–13
    Community Land Trust campaigns,
        33, 116, 134
    financial independence of, 90
    Living Wage campaigns of, 12, 77–78
    London Muslim Centre campaign,
        39–40, 119
    Newham General Hospital cam-
        paign, 77–78
    relationships within, 119
    "Strangers into Citizens" campaign,
        132–33
tension, 31–33, 73–74, 99
terrorism. *See* extremism
Theology of Community Organising, A
    (Shanahan), 78–80
Theory of Justice, A (Rawls), 160n2
Tocqueville, Alexis de, 64, 65
Tower Hamlets, x, 116, 122, 123, 129
trade unions (mediating civil
    institutions)
    in community organizing, 56, 88
    community organizing's challenge to,
        153
    diversity in, 46
    in Living Wage campaigns, 12
    role in democracies, 11, 71
    and wedge issues, 100
traditions
    in liberalism, 149
    mediating power, 144
    pluralism of, 139
    political theories on, 137–39
    in populism, 143–45
    resisting commodification, 151
    of Secular Humanism, 51, 152,
        157n24
    valued by the poorest, 149
    varieties of, 139–40

Trump, Donald, 13
    approach to governance, 71–72
    divisive rhetoric of, 1–2, 16, 116–17
    elite status of, 9
    factors in victory of, 15–16, 72,
        74–75, 82–83, 114, 116–18, 148
    fake populism of, 142, 147–48, 150
    and Pope Francis, 153
    presidential campaign of, 1, 9
    racism of, 82–83, 162n18

United Kingdom Independence Party,
    114
United Power for Action and Justice,
    56–58
urbanization, 2–3
usury (exploitative lending), 24, 93–96,
    100, 149

values
    in community organizing, 77
    impact of liberalism on, 10, 64
    in integration policy, 105–7
    in negotiated pluralism, 107–9
    of religious institutions, 77
    role in motivation, 36–37
    See also *convictions*; good, concep-
        tions of
voluntarism, 63–64

wages. *See* jobs and wages
Wahabi regime (Saudi Arabia), 9
"War on Wonga" campaign, 168n3
Warren, Elizabeth, 117
Warsi, Sayeeda, 158n1
Watson, Jenny, 166n26
Wax, Lynn, 48
Webb, Julie, 48
We Can Win (campaigning organi-
    zation), 165n14
wedge issues, 75–76, 99–102, 132
"We Don't Want a Miracle, We
    Just Want a Sign" campaign,
    42–43
Welby, Justin (archbishop of Canter-
    bury), 108–9, 168n3

Whose Justice? Which Rationality?
(MacIntyre), 139
Williams, Rowan (archbishop of Canterbury), 107–8
Wolin, Sheldon, 65, 144–45
women
on abortion issue, 101–2
inadequate representation in the Church, 164n47
in Muslim communities, 122–25
women's marches, 2, 75
Women and Equalities Select Committee (House of Commons), 124–25
Wonga (payday lender), 93–94
working class communities
alienated by progressive identity politics, 118
and Brexit, 114–15
challenges of organizing in, 115
commonalities of, 148–49
failures of the left in, 13–15, 16
and immigration policy, 131–32
and integration tensions, 23, 113–16
the Occupy movements and, 144
ressentiment of, 143
support for right-wing populism, 16
and Trump's victory, 82–83

Yeltsin, Boris, 1
Yvette (Congolese migrant), 112–13

Angus Ritchie heads the Centre for Theology and Community in London. He is a Church of England priest and the author of *From Morality to Metaphysics: The Theistic Implications of Our Ethical Commitments.*

CPSIA information can be obtained
at www.ICGtesting.com
Printed in the USA
LVHW081259260919
632360LV00014B/414/P